DIGITAL
DIVERSITY

DIGITAL
DIVERSITY

Youth, Equity, and Information Technology

E. Dianne Looker and

Ted D. Naylor, editors

Wilfrid Laurier University Press

This book has been published with the help of a grant from the Canadian Federation for the Humanities and Social Sciences, through the Aid to Scholarly Publications Programme, using funds provided by the Social Sciences and Humanities Research Council of Canada. We acknowledge the financial support of the Canada Book Fund for our publishing activities.

Library and Archives Canada Cataloguing in Publication

Digital diversity : youth, equity, and information technology /E. Dianne Looker and Ted D. Naylor, editors.

Includes bibliographical references and index.
Also available in electronic format.
ISBN 978-1-55458-185-6

1. Technology and youth—Canada. 2. Educational technology—Canada. 3. Computer literacy—Canada. I. Looker, Ellen Dianne II. Naylor, Ted D. (Ted Dewar), [date]

LC149.5.D54 2010   373.133'4   C2010-900910-X

ISBN 978-1-55458-203-7
Electronic format.

1. Technology and youth—Canada. 2. Educational technology—Canada. 3. Computer literacy—Canada. I. Looker, Ellen Dianne II. Naylor, Ted D. (Ted Dewar), [date]

LC149.5.D54 2010a   373.133'4   C2010-900911-8

Cover design by David Drummond using images from Shutterstock. Text design by Brenda Prangley.

© 2010 Wilfrid Laurier University Press
Waterloo, Ontario, Canada
www.wlupress.wlu.ca

This book is printed on FSC recycled paper and is certified Ecologo. It is made from 100% post-consumer fibre, processed chlorine free, and manufactured using biogas energy.

Printed in Canada

Every reasonable effort has been made to acquire permission for copyright material used in this text, and to acknowledge all such indebtedness accurately. Any errors and omissions called to the publisher's attention will be corrected in future printings.

Recycled
Supporting responsible use
of forest resources
FSC   www.fsc.org Cert no. SGS-COC-003153
© 1996 Forest Stewardship Council

Table of Contents

List of Tables
and Figures

LIST OF TABLES

LIST OF FIGURES

Chapter 1

Introduction

E. Dianne Looker

Ted D. Naylor

This book is about youth. The focus on youth reflects our recognition that young people are at the forefront of change as we move more solidly into the twenty-first century. They are initiating and developing change through regular access and use of technology in ways that are thought to be novel in relation to previous generations. In addition, youth are more deeply affected than older age groups by some of the key changes taking place, including the incredible proliferation of computers and the increasingly heavy use of the Internet for both information sharing and for communication.

We are interested in understanding how the tools and resources provided by information and communication technology (ICT) are made available to young people and how different groups of youth do (or don't) develop facility and competence with this technology. Many argue that computers constitute the "new literacy" (Snyder 1998), at least for youth. This belief is reflected in the incredible investments that have been made in ICT in schools. Giving all students access to this technology and the skills to use it effectively is seen as key to Canada's success in the global, "information-based" economy. The questions we address in this book include how this access varies for different groups of youth, which young people develop facility with ICT, and what impact this technology has had on their learning and their lives.

The term "information and communication technology" can cover a wide range of technologies, from telephones and televisions to text messaging on cell phones. Because of our interest in the link between government policies on ICT and education, we are focusing on just the two related components of ICT that we believe are most central to teaching and learning practices: computers and the Internet.

We are interested in how and where youth use these technologies and what impact these technologies have for different subgroups of youth while recognizing also that youth have an impact on the development and use of technology. We are also interested in how these technologies are being used within the domain of education, and how student teachers and current teachers are using technology for educational purposes and routine classroom use.

Throughout the book, contributors are critical of the linkages made between technology and fundamental change in either the education system or pedagogical outcomes. Accordingly, we draw attention to how technology is actually being used by educators, students, and teachers. To date, use remains largely at the level of low skills and tasks, not deeply integrated into curriculum and pedagogy as originally imagined by proponents of ICT integrated education. We argue that what is required, in part, is a more systemic educational and pedagogical consensus around the links between ICT, teaching practices, and educational outcomes.

This book developed out of a larger research project, the Equity and Technology Research Alliance.[1] A research alliance involves a close partnership between one or more universities (in this case Acadia, Dalhousie, and Mount Saint Vincent Universities) and one or more government departments or community groups. For this project the key research partners were the departments of education in Nunavut and Nova Scotia. Several other partners facilitated in the research in various ways (see the project website archived at http://techequity.acadiau.ca for details).

As the name suggests the Equity and Technology project involved examining equity issues with respect to technology. That is, we were interested in whether, how, and for whom these new technologies allowed traditionally marginalized youth to participate more fully in the new global economy. If there is to be equity in the use of technology, there need to be opportunities for youth not only to access the technology but also for them to learn the skills and develop the confidence to use this technology effectively. Equity can mean the extent to which this access, and the opportunities for the development of skill and competence, is independent of the young person's social location. Beyond this, however, the equity issues we consider look at how and whether ICT is, in fact, able to help disadvantaged youth overcome some of their disadvantages (for example, by reducing the negative effects of distance from an urban centre for rural youth).

As we outline in the proposal for the research, "In a multi-cultural society ICT has the potential to be an equity enhancing resource. Canada's economy depends upon the inclusion of youth who can harness ICT in ways that build upon their distinctive cultural knowledge and that serve their economic interests" (Looker 2003, 1). The question we ask is how ICT is used to gather and share information and to facilitate communication—the two main functions of "information" and "communication" technology. More specifically we are interested in the role of schools, and other institutions that work with youth, in making this technology and the skills to use it available to youth who would otherwise be excluded.

THEORETICAL PERSPECTIVES

In order to make sense of how subgroups of youth who differ in their cultural background and social location access and use ICT, we draw on the work of Pierre Bourdieu and others and on their concepts of human and social capital.

It is generally accepted that *human capital* is located within an individual. The various "skills, competencies, and qualifications" (Schuller 2007, 18; see also Conrad 2007) that individuals develop through formal and informal learning constitute their human capital. They take this capital with them as they move through different life stages. This capital is not transferable, except in circumstances where someone teaches others their skills and thereby increases the human capital of these others (without decreasing that of the teacher). An interesting characteristic of human capital is that it tends to increase as it is used; that is, as one applies one's skills, these skills are solidified and increased. Indeed, unlike economic capital, human capital declines if left unused over periods of time (Krahn 1997).

There have been a number of definitions of *social capital*, because this concept is embraced by different social science disciplines. These differing definitions are, not surprisingly, associated with controversies about what is and isn't (or what should and shouldn't be) included in this concept. Without going into the debate in detail, it is useful to highlight some of the key positions in this discussion.

Halpern (2005) defines social capital as "social networks and the norms and sanctions that govern their character." This is similar to Putnam's (2000) definition that focuses on social networks and the norms of reciprocity and trustworthiness that arise from them. The definition used by van Staveren (2003, 415) focuses on "a shared commitment to social values as expressed in the quantity and quality of social relationships." Lin (2000, 786) defines it as "investment and use of embedded resources in social relations for expected return." The notion of "expected returns" is contested by some, who note that "the more explicit and instrumental the approach is, the less it resembles social capital, which is understood in terms of shared values and reciprocity" (Schuller 2007, 24). In other words, the expectation is that one enters into a relationship for the sake of the relationship not in order to benefit oneself in terms of payoffs down the road. Coleman (1988) defines social capital by its function, as a resource that can be drawn upon, as does Conrad (2007): "social capital [is] a resource comprised of the benefits of social connections and relationships." These definitions are similar to the one used by the Canadian based Policy Research Institute (PRI), which states that "the networks of social ties that a person or group call upon for resources and support constitute their social capital" (2005, 1). We have adopted a definition very close to that of the PRI: *social capital is the network of social ties that a person or group can call upon for resources and support.*

Scholars of social capital often differentiate between two types of social capital, referred to as bonding and bridging social capital[2] (Nooteboom 2007; Schuller 2007). Bonding social capital connects people who are similar to each other. Bridging social capital refers to connections people make with dissimilar others. Bonding capital tends to occur among members of a closely knit, homogenous community, strengthening their ties of "thick trust" (Pigg and Crank 2004) and of reciprocity with each other. Bridging social capital, on the other hand, tends to be external to one's community, creating links with diverse others (Alkalimat and Williams 2001; Pigg and Crank 2004).

Much of the existing literature portrays bridging social capital as more positive, leading to the development of skills necessary for employment and mobility in today's complex world (Narayan 1999). Bonding social capital, on the other hand, has been presented in more negative terms, often linked to multicultural societies, where individuals may pay closer attention to tribal, ethnic, or political allegiances to their own groups rather than national or plural interests (Daniel, Schweir and McCalla 2003; Norris 2003). What is more, bonding ties may become obligatory, rather than voluntary, and lead to resentment, especially if overused (Bezanson 2006). As Gaved and Anderson (2006) observe, bonding capital assists individuals in "getting by," while bridging capital assists individuals in "getting ahead." We would caution, however, that for some groups development of bonding social capital within the group is essential to their cultural survival. This caution is reinforced in Gaved and Anderson's (2006, 7) model, in which bonding social capital is expected to increase the subjective quality of life, while bridging social capital is thought to primarily increase the objective quality of life.

Further, some scholars believe that there can be negative effects of both bridging and bonding social capital. Nooteboom (2007) recognizes that bonding may inhibit learning and innovation (and lead to such things as price fixing among economic organizations), while bridging can risk dependence: "When dependence is strong and asymmetric, relationships can become repressive" (2007, 34). And even bridging social networks can be exclusionary (Leonard 2004).

Others see the two types as dependent on each other. So, Schuller (2007, 15) argues that "one can have bonding social capital without bridging, but not vice versa." On the other hand, Leonard (2004) claims that bridging can undermine bonding when it disrupts the trust at the local level, which feeds on distrust of wider institutions and "outside" groups. In their empirical study of bridging and bonding social capital, Kim, Subramanian, and Kawachi (2006) find bridging and bonding to be inversely related. So, for example, when individual members of disadvantaged groups form bonds with those from more advantaged backgrounds, it may further their own mobility ("getting ahead") while undermining their ties with their traditional community. According to Lin (2000), bridging social capital often comes at the cost of reducing one's recognition within and identity with a group.

More than one scholar has noted that there are inequities reinforced, if not created, through activities that strengthen social capital. Central to these analyses are the ways that gender inequity is exacerbated. It often falls to women to maintain the ties within a community or family group, to perform the work in building and preserving relationships, including voluntary work (van Staveren 2003). As Wellman (2001) puts it, women do most of the "network." Lin (2000) notes that males and females often have different sorts of social capital; males have stronger ties to core organizations that benefit them more, while the links females have tend to be to those in more peripheral positions. Racial groups can also vary in the extent to which they access kin and non-kin networks, and the extent to which these networks provide them with resources that can be translated into other forms of capital (Lin 2000).

Perhaps more important is to recognize that there are different forms of social capital (bridging and bonding) and that there are optimal levels of each for individuals and groups in different social situations (Nooteboom 2007). What is more, the "forms of social capital and the relative importance of bonding and bridging for any given social community will change over time, so that there is rarely a stable equilibrium (and where it exists it will be time limited" (Nooteboom 2007, 17). The bonds that link individuals and groups can be overused (leading to resentment) or can lapse due to under-use—that is, when not reinforced through contact and communication (Bezanson 2006). In this project we explore how different groups use ICT to maintain this contact and communication, and what effect ICT has on their development of various forms of capital, recognizing that this effect may well be neutral or negative (Angrist and Lavy 2002; Cuban 2001; Fuchs and Woessmann 2004).

A key component of "capital" is the fact that it involves investment—the "allocation of resources that might have been used otherwise" (Schuller 2007, 23). Recognizing this component makes it clear that a focus on capital is relevant to analyses of ICT use. Access to, use of and skill development with ICT involves incredible investment of money (by governments, families and individuals), as well as considerable time and effort (by families, schools, youth organizations and individuals). These resources certainly could have been used other ways - so the issue of who benefits from these investments and what pay offs there are from them becomes all the more important to ensure marginalized populations could enjoy all of the benefits, both economic and educational, of ICT and their apparent advantages.

Another important aspect of "capital" is its convertibility; that is the ability of those with high levels of capital in one sphere (such as cultural capital) to be able to transform that capital into another (such as economic capital). "Like resources in general, it is not social capital itself but the services it can render that yield advantage" (Nooteboom 2007, 33). It has been said that Bourdieu (1986), one of the scholars who has written extensively about forms of capital, focuses primarily on conversion to economic capital (Leonard 2004). Our interest goes beyond this. For example, if those with certain types of social capital are better able to develop skills (human capital) this is an important conversion worthy of attention. The question then becomes not only who has access to various forms of capital but how convertible this capital is, for whom, and under what circumstances.

THE RELEVANCE OF ICT

Our focus on ICT reflects our interest in the ways that it is used to enhance the capital resources available to youth by providing them access to information (thereby potentially improving their human capital) and by allowing them to communicate effectively over a widely dispersed area with their social network (thereby maintaining and enhancing their social capital). Of course, if the proponents of ICT as central to the "new literacy" are correct, then knowledge of how to effectively use this technology in itself enhances a person's human capital. Certainly, heavy investments in ICT have been made, and are being made, by individuals, families and governments at all levels. The question is, what effect is this investment having on the experiences and development of human and social capital of youth, both advantaged and disadvantaged?

One of the key aspects of ICT is that it involves *communication* technologies. It allows people to make linkages; it facilitates communication between individuals and between groups. The Internet is a key component of ICT that is used for communication purposes, and so in parts of our analysis we examine use of the Internet separately from general ICT use. It is, of course, not the only technology used for communication. Although we have little data in this project on cell phones, these certainly are used more and more for communication. Individuals share information in other ways—burning and sharing CDs and DVDs, writing and printing documents that are then shared, and using data projectors to present a variety of documents and files, with printed words, sounds, and images (not to mention "old-fashioned technology": phones, radios, and television).

However, a key difference between the Internet and more traditional communication media is the way connections are made. "The Internet's unique ability for interconnection, its many-to-many approach, compared to radio's one-to-many approach, coupled with its decentralized, emancipatory, and immediacy features, makes it a far more powerful tool for developing horizontal networks of communication, collaboration, and potential mobilization than either radio or television" (Dale and Naylor 2005, 217). Wellman (2001) emphasizes the shift from place-to-place communication (that characterizes not only radio and television but also land line telephones and desktop computers) to person-to-person communication that can be separated from a spatial location. Cell phones, laptops, and other portable devices that can access the Internet have lead to a "mobile-ization" of communication.

Part of the reason that there is so much interest in ICT, especially computers and the Internet, is this communication function. Being able to use ICT to communicate in various settings is seen as critical for participation in the so-called "information society." ICT has the potential "to bring together dispersed members of familial or ethnic groups" (Wilson and Peterson 2002, 449). According to Dutta-Bergman (2005, 104), "technology acts as a community builder, a facilitator of communication among community members and an access point for securing information, a critical resource in the current environment."

Although there is some agreement that online communication is best when it supplements face-to-face interaction (Wellman et al. 1996), the Internet adds several other dimensions. "Computer mediated communication supplements, arranges and amplifies in-person and telephone communications rather than replacing them" (Wellman 2001, 242). The asynchronous nature of Internet communication provides flexibility and "gives participants more control over timing and content of their self disclosures. This allows role-to-role relationships to develop from shared interests rather than be stunted at the outset by differences in social status" (Wellman 2001, 246). It allows individuals to access communities of interest "rather than the compulsory tolerance of people you often do not like forced on you by proximity" (Coleman 1988, 100). By its very nature, the Internet allows the creation of "networks for dialogue, as opposed to merely receiving messages through communication media such as television and radio" (Dale and Naylor 2005, 215). Technologies afford possibilities for social relations and social structures (Wellman 2001) and so provide opportunities for both individuals and the multiple communities (Wilson and Peterson 2002) of which they are members. These technologies have "afforded greater connectivity between communities. The ease of communication to a large number of people facilitates ties that cut across group boundaries" (Wellman 2001, 247).

ICT is not just a communication technology, however. It is also a technology that is used, particularly by the education system, for accessing, storing, sharing and analyzing *information*. Educational software abounds that provides detailed information about a wide variety of topics relevant to the school curriculum. Computer-based tutorials allow students to learn a range of skills. Beyond the capabilities of stand-alone computers, the Internet provides access to an ever-increasing store of material—material that can be and is used by teachers as well as by the young people in their classrooms. The potential of ICT for enhancing equity among disadvantaged youth is seen in the availability of this online universe. If all youth have equal access to information that is relevant to their development of human capital or, minimally, their ability to obtain useful educational credentials, then the playing field is reasonably level. If, however, some youth are better able to access relevant information, if they have the skills to effectively search the Internet while others struggle with the mass of material they find, then the social divisions become deeper.

These divisions based on ICT access and use are called the "digital divide." Before examining the results from our studies it is worthwhile highlighting some recent developments in educational and government policy as well as research findings relating to this well-documented digital divide.

EDUCATION POLICY AND ICT

Since the 1980s an international policy discourse surrounding education and training has emerged in advanced social democracies (Lloyd and Payne 2003). A central thrust behind this discourse is the notion of "knowledge economies" emerging in tight competition with one another. This competition is played out through the now global pressures of the market, where states must compete on economic terms, exploiting the commercial advantages offered by a more autonomous, well-educated, and flexible workforce (Lloyd and Payne 2003). In this vein, new growth theory has been very influential in highlighting the role of education in creating human capital and in the production of new knowledge and "education-related externalities" (Peters 2003). The intensification of global competition, coupled with the rapid proliferation and acceleration of advanced information communication technologies (ICT) have combined to form the basis of a new global order and competitive environment (see OECD 1996) and to create new demands on educational policy and practice.

The roots of this educational policy discourse and practice, though diverse, stem from the 1970s onward. A complex interplay has developed between the state and the corporate sector, which involves actively seeking out new ways to (re)organize the functions and welfare/distribution capacities of the state, increasingly through market-orientated outcomes and deliverables. Within the economic/production sphere, the overall paradigm shift was generally described as "post-Fordist," in an attempt to capture new production factors both at the point of production and within the restructuring of the capital/labour nexus. Within the sphere of the nation-state, the paradigm shift was categorized as "post-Keynesian" in an attempt to capture new relationships between both capital and the state and within the restructuring of the citizen/state nexus. An eventual convergence of private- and public-sector management theory provided the tenets of a "new managerialism" (Gewirtz and Ball 2000) and offered concrete mechanisms of change, culminating in new regimes of accountability and transparency for the dynamics of state and social welfare expenditures. E-Government initiatives sought to leverage technology to tighten the service relationship among citizens and the state, while at the same time ICTs were thought to offer the state strategies for the potential inclusion of marginalized groups in the processes of governance.

Alongside these trends, a new discourse of public policy evolved, offering new ways to speak of and conceptualize the role of the welfare state within a complex but discernable trajectory of neo-liberal modes of governance. Although the trajectory, complexity, and ramifications of these developments have been different across advanced industrialized countries, attention to measuring educational outcomes in relation to their economic contribution has been a common development, with a focus on education's contribution to developing human capital for the knowledge economy. At the same time, the notion of the digital divide loosely prompted an attempt to ensure marginalized populations could take advantage of all the benefits, economic and educational, of ICT.

Critically bound up within the current literature and research on educational policy and program, then, has been the roles that these advanced technologies have played. This is particularly important since ICT has typically been understood as the main catalyst for changes in the socio-economic order (see Braverman 1974; Zuboff 1989; Castells 1996/2001; 1998; 2001). In the field of economics, there has also been a growing theoretical consensus that the driving force behind economic growth is technological advancement, an assertion that has clearly found its way into public-policy formulation and practice for many governments, including Canada. In this way, globalization and technology are understood as hermetically intertwined, based on the contention that the "rapid development, diffusion and utilization of ICT has profoundly affected the modes of global economic production as well as consumption" (Parayil 2005, 41).

Indeed, in what is recognized as one of the key empirically based discussions on ICT and globalization to date, Castell's (1996/2001, 13) *Network Society* states: "The information technology revolution was instrumental in allowing the implementation of a fundamental process of restructuring of the capitalist system from the 1980s onward." The transformation of the "material" mode of production is based on the often-taken-for-granted emergence of knowledge as the most important factor of production, surpassing land, labour, and capital, based on the diffusion of ICT throughout the social order (Parayil 2005).

Now a ubiquitous term of popular media, business, and government, the term "knowledge economy" attempts to describe a potentially new process where *knowledge about technology* and levels of information flow become crucial to economic development, accounting for differential growth patterns globally (Peters 2003). One result is that economic policies increasingly evaluate the merit of knowledge from an economic perspective, as opposed to a fundamental social good (Keyway and Robb 2004). Indeed, the recent scholarship and focus on creating and harnessing human capital is an explicit attempt to capture the connection between labour and capital within a reconfigured socio-economic landscape. As the OECD report *The Knowledge-based Economy* (1996, 7) stated over a decade ago, "Governments will need more stress on upgrading human capital through promoting access to a range of skills ... enhancing the knowledge distribution power of the economy through collaborative networks and the diffusion of technology."

From a federal policy and program perspective, Canada has aggressively positioned itself as a leading proponent of the knowledge economy, making massive investments in infrastructure and programs based on the understanding that Canada needs to continue to develop and utilize its highly skilled workforce to remain competitive and develop human capital within a global and increasingly knowledge-based economy (OECD 2004). For example, in Nova Scotia, from a provincial policy and program perspective, the province is attempting to competitively position itself as a leader in the knowledge economy. The province has undertaken an initiative to ensure that every Nova Scotian will have broadband access to the Internet (Nova Scotia 2007), a goal it is still working to achieve.[3] This strategy is being advanced alongside a host of initiatives focusing on growing the ICT sector in Nova Scotia. For instance, the province is actively advertising itself as a "near-shore" destination for the global IT marketplace based on its highly skilled and flexible labour pool, particularly its university-educated labour pool (see novascotia business.com). It has also recently created a dedicated information and communications job site (techportjobs.com), which links recent graduates, local professionals, and expatriates with employment opportunities in Nova Scotia.

Within this broad socio-economic policy context, there is now a significant contention that lack of *literacy with ICT* represents a major obstacle for both capital and labour in advanced economies if Canada is to compete globally in a knowledge economy. Within Canada alone, for instance, we have witnessed an incredible mix of resources and efforts aimed at increasing ICT literacy in education within the past decade. As Milton (2005, 3) contends: "The early drivers of levels of investment in ICT in education have not changed. ICT skills are a key factor in both individuals' success in the labour market and in national economic growth." Implicit with the massive investment in ICT infrastructure, education, and training is a belief that ICT literacy is fundamental to a successful socio-economic sphere in an age of "informational capitalism" (Parayil 2005).

Although this book is not specifically about ICT literacy, it does begin with the assumption that ICT is now positioned, for better or worse, at the critical intersections between public policy, education, equity, and the ability of individuals to successfully prosper economically. The contributors to this book explore how different groups and populations actually *use* technology in relation to broader, often tacit yet powerful, assumptions around the need to understand and use ICT to obtain educational and economic success for individuals and communities, but particularly for youth. By paying attention to the empirical outcomes and actual use as well as the understandings of ICT by youth and those teaching youth (i.e., educators), the book highlights the current gaps in policy between ICT use, education, and equity. In these ways it challenges many of the current and taken-for-granted linkages that are naturally assumed between ICT and youth.

From an educational perspective, the different parts of the book taken together suggest that there is a widening gap between the rhetoric around the importance of ICT for education, on the one hand, and how teachers, student teachers, and students are actually using ICT in routine classroom settings, on the other (Angrist and Lavy 2002; Stoll, 2000; Zwaagstra 2008).

From an equity perspective, the analyses presented here suggest that ICT is not a panacea. Rather, ICT is used for strikingly different ends by different groups, including cultural, street, and gender-based populations, as well as "equity groups" targeted for government interventions. As ICT continues to be positioned as a critical enabler for equity among and between groups, researchers and policy officials must begin to confront the data and build evidence about how ICT is *actually* being used, as opposed to only a consideration about how it *should* be used—a task this book takes up and a challenge we wish to put to other researchers.

To this end, it is important for any analysis or policy initiative to recognize that there are important differences in use, skill levels, and objectives in using ICT throughout the social order. These differences should not, and do not, necessarily follow along a hierarchal ordering of "lower" and "higher" skills. It is not simply a matter of "dumb" users of technology and "smart" users of technology when considering how individuals employ ICT in ways that matter to their lives, circumstances, and needs. Rather the issue becomes how ICT is used in ways that meet the needs and goals of disparate subgroups of youth.

THE DIGITAL DIVIDES IN CANADA

In order to document these issues of access and use of ICT there has been extensive research on and overviews of the so-called digital divide in Canada (Looker and Thiessen 2003; Reddick, Boucher, and Groseilliers 2000; Rideout 2000). An important point to note in any discussion of digital divides is that the between-country divides are large, often larger than within-country divides. Chinn and Fairlie (2007) document some sizeable cross-country differences in the penetration of computers and the Internet. Two points are relevant from their analysis. One is that Canada (like the US) fares well in these comparisons. Based on 2001 data, there are 61.1 computers per 100 people in Canada (compared to Sub-Saharan Africa with 1.0). About a half of the population in North America has Internet access (compared to 16.5% in Europe and Central Asia and one half of one percent in South Asia). However, since age is also a major predictor of access and use (Cuneo 2002; OECD 2001; Reddick, Boucher, and Groseilliers 2000; Rideout 2000) differences among youth may be less pronounced (Corbett and Willms 2002). Nevertheless, any analysis of the digital divide in Canada has to recognize this more global context.

The most common focus of the literature on the digital divide is on access to technology, that is, whether a person or household has a computer and connections to the Internet. As we note above, however, and as others emphasize (Attewell 2001; Natriello 2001), it is also important to consider the extent to which individuals develop confidence and skills with the technology and how they actually use it.

There are various social characteristics that have been identified as contributing to these divides.[4] Much of this research is reviewed in Looker and Thiessen (2003) and will not be repeated here. Their conclusion, based on an analysis of some Statistics Canada data sets is that: "Many of the sub-group differences in use of and attitudes toward ICT are fairly small, and there seem to be possibilities for further reducing them" (Looker and Thiessen 2003, 21).

Home access is consistently found to be important for youth (Corbett and Willms 2002; Looker and Thiessen 2002; Looker and Thiessen 2003; Thiessen and Looker 2007). Cost is a constraint, especially for youth (Reddick and Boucher 2002); however, school and public access can compensate in important ways for lack of home access (Reddick and Boucher 2002; Looker and Thiessen 2003). "There is a continuing demand and need for public access and training in both rural and urban locations in Canada for those who do not have, or cannot afford, home access" (Reddick and Boucher 2002, 30).

The situation is even more challenging for ethnic and racial minorities, especially First Nations groups. This is documented further in chapter 3 by Thiessen and Looker. Although almost all First Nations schools have computers and Internet access (Plante 2005), access for students is more limited than in other schools. Further, resources for teacher training and for language-appropriate software are also more restricted (Plante, 2005). Although some programs specifically target First Nations schools and youth, Downing (2002) notes that these programs are frequently unstable. Gender differences in access tend to be more subtle, but research has shown that they persist (Chinn and Fairlie 2007; Looker 2007). Given the very different experiences of young women and men in schools, attention to the gender divide is still warranted. What is more, as chapter 4 by Campbell and Henning notes, these gender differences in the use of ICT often advantage males, but sometimes advantage females. These findings suggest that more nuanced analyses and discussions of digital divides are warranted.

Given the rate at which ICT penetration is changing (Sciadas 2002), ongoing research is needed. Computers and the Internet are relatively new technologies (especially when compared to telephones, radio, or television). Diffusion patterns are changing. When we consider the other divides that exist in Canada based on income, education, gender, location, and so on, it is likely that there will be corresponding divides in access and use of ICT. In light of the emphasis placed on ICT literacy, especially for youth, it is critical that we understand the nature and effects of these divides. Documenting these divides and their effects is one of the tasks of this book.

DATA SOURCES

Our focus on equity and potentially marginalized youth led us to undertake various activities to gather information about access to, use of, and skill with ICT in various subgroups of youth. These included numerous meetings and discussions with participating partners and members of community groups and the analysis of several data sets gathered by Statistics Canada, as well as the gathering of our own data through focus groups and interviews with key players and formal surveys with high school students, teachers, student teachers in faculties of education, and youth in alternative schools. Having information from such a diverse set of stakeholders is rare and valuable for our analysis. It is the information from the data we collected that is presented in this book. If one is interested in questions relating to ICT and equity, one key question is that of access—the issue of the digital divide. Although the digital divide is discussed and documented in this book, it is not the only or indeed the main focus. To quote our proposal: "This project is more than another analysis of the digital divide. It involves an integrated analysis of cross-cutting divides; it examines new dimensions including how ICT is learned in different settings; it looks at how ICT skill and facility (or lack thereof) affect other aspects of youth's lives" (Looker 2003, 1).

Our research is also fairly unique given the groups it includes. Most of the so-called nationally representative data sets collected by Statistics Canada omit the far north—a region of Canada that is increasing in strategic and cultural importance. These same data sets rarely have information on First Nations youth living on reserves. Surveys that include African Canadians are equally rare, and even more unusual is to have data on and from street youth. All these groups are included in the research reported in the following chapters.

Why these groups? We chose these groups partly to counter the gaps in the existing literature, but we also chose the minority groups strategically. Further, we chose to focus our data collection efforts to two regions of Canada:

Nova Scotia and Nunavut. Part of this choice reflects the fact that the project was a Research Alliance and so was driven not solely by the academic researchers, but also by the central partners, the departments of education in these two jurisdictions. The choice also allowed us to meet a number of our research objectives. Given the communication function of ICT, we wanted to include rural and remote areas not yet covered by high-speed connections in addition to better-serviced urban centres to see whether ICT has, indeed, meant the "death of distance" (Cairncross 1997).

In terms of cultural groups, we wanted the ability to contrast different structural situations. The Mi'kmaq in Nova Scotia, like other First Nations groups in Canada, have official status and separate educational facilities on their formal reserves. African Canadians are no less marginalized than First Nations youth in Nova Scotia, but they have no such official status, and so there is no official government mandate to specifically address their needs. If government policies and initiatives are effective, we should see the differential impact on these different groups. Finally, the Inuit in Nunavut have a fairly unique situation. Although they are a small minority in Canada as a whole, in Nunavut (as in the other northern territories) they are very much a majority. What is more, in addition to official recognition of the Inuit under the Land Claims Agreement, the Nunavut government has a clear and explicit mandate to preserve and strengthen Inuit culture and languages while ensuring their citizens are not isolated and marginalized in the Canadian and world economies.

THE CONTEXT

In order for the reader to better understand the material presented in this book, it is important that we set the context. Since fewer readers are likely to be familiar with Nunavut, more detail will be provided on that region, although the analysis of data from Nunavut is restricted to chapters 2, 3, and 4.

Nunavut, one of the three northern territories of Canada, is going through some dramatic transformations. It is a sparsely populated region (with a population of about 30,000 people spread out over 20% of Canada's land mass). There are no roads between the twenty-five communities that are spread across the territory. Travel (other than out on the land for traditional hunting and fishing) is by plane most months of the year and by boat for the two months in the summer when waterways are accessible. Given the incredible expense of air travel, these facts mean that communities are separated in ways that are hard for those from the south to comprehend. In light of the remote nature of these communities (many of which were artificially created by the Canadian government in the 1950s to establish and maintain Canadian sovereignty over the Arctic) communication between those in different locales becomes all the more challenging—hence the potential for ICT to help bridge these gaps.

The Nunavut Government is young, having officially existed only since 1999, and is faced with the challenge of trying to develop policies on a wide range of issues. At the same time, with finite resources, it must address the same challenges facing administrations in more established regions as Canada moves to a more knowledge-based society. There is widespread recognition that Nunavut communities need to become more involved in the global economy while still honouring and integrating their traditional values and knowledge, reflected in the policy of *Inuit Qaujimajatuqanginnik* (IQ).

A fundamental objective in the creation of Nunavut for the Inuit was to reclaim their land, their culture, and their language. What role can and does ICT play in these efforts? How can ICT be incorporated in ways that serve the policy objectives and cultural values of this new government? As a communication tool this technology, especially the Internet, has the potential to facilitate collaborative efforts and consensus building across distance. For example, the school and a non-governmental agency working with the school in Sanikiluaq have set up a local television station that is broadcast to all households in the community (personal communication with the principal, Sanikiluaq). These broadcasts regularly carry community notices, but they also involve discussions of Elders talking with Elders. These live discussions are taped and then played back to the whole community. This example shows the potential for ICT to be used for consultation and communication within a community; the question is how practical such procedures are between communities. What are the ways that ICT can facilitate local communities reaching their goals?

When the government of Nunavut was being formed, the decision was made to distribute government offices throughout the territory rather than concentrating them in the capital. Distributing government offices in this way means that communication is a critical issue not only from government to communities but also within government departments. ICT provides an important communication venue, but one that is limited without high-speed connections[5] (personal communication with member of Nunavut Department of Education).

As a skill relevant to a knowledge-based economy, ICT is seen as being critical particularly for youth. However, many schools in Nunavut are limited in the extent to which they are able to use ICT in the classroom. Internet access is so slow that there is often a "time out" before relevant material can be downloaded, so searches on the Internet become impractical (personal communication with teacher, Arviat). Few teachers have training in ICT, and there is very little ICT-oriented curriculum available (personal communication with teacher, Pangnirtung). Given these constraints, youth in Nunavut are in danger of falling behind in their development of ICT-related skills, relative to their counterparts in the south.

Like schools and communities in the south of Canada, schools and communities in Nunavut are wired; they have computers and Internet connections for their students, teachers, and community members. Indeed, some Nunavut schools have a higher student-to-computer ratio than elsewhere in Canada (personal communication with principal, Resolute Bay). Many but not all communities have public access sites in schools and libraries or those made available through the Nunavut Arctic College; however, in some sites these computers are outdated (personal communication with teacher, Rankin Inlet), and others require technical support that is only rarely available, given the vast distances and limited resources (personal communication with teacher, Pangnirtung). For all but those in the capital of Iqaluit, the current Internet connection speed is painfully slow and access to the Internet can be erratic at best (Looker, 2004).

According to a recent Statistics Canada report (Plante and Beattie 2004, Table C-1) schools in Nunavut are much less likely than those elsewhere in Canada (8% in Nunavut versus 16% Canada-wide) to say they had high-speed Internet connections in the school year 2003–2004; only 57% of Nunavut schools reported having a formal ICT policy (compared to 91% of schools Canada-wide). Many communities in Nunavut still rely on costly dial-up connections, resulting in long-distance charges for every use (personal communication with teacher, Arviat). As a result, rates of use of the Internet are much lower than is true in other regions of Canada (Plante and Beattie, 2004).

There are a number of non-technical barriers to ICT use as well, and these must be considered before use of ICT in Nunavut can be understood. As Rideout notes, there is little locally relevant content on the Internet for remote rural areas (2000, 8), so the information there may have less appeal (see also Looker and Thiessen 2002; 2003). Traditionally the Inuit (who constitute 85% of Nunavut's population) emphasize face-to-face contact, respect for Elders, consensus making, and the spoken rather than the written word. In addition to the fact that for many Inuit English (the dominant language of the Internet) is a second language, there a number of different dialects in Nunavut. In the Kitikmeot region, Innuinaqtun, which uses Roman orthography, is the traditional dialect. In the Kivalliq and Qikiqtani regions the syllabic-based Inuktitut is used, but there are several versions of Inuktitut; so south Baffin is different from north Baffin, which is different again from the "mainland" or from Sanikiluaq on the Belcher Islands. Such variations create challenges to communication across distances. Many teachers, especially at the high schools, and government officials are *quallunaat* (non-Inuit). They often have little training to prepare them for the cultural issues in the north and they often stay for only a year or two, resulting in high teacher turnover (personal communication).

A counter to some of these challenges is the Inuit tradition of embracing new technologies if these technologies can facilitate their activities, so long as they do not undermine important aspects of their traditional culture. At a meeting between representatives of the Nunavut Department of Education and Elders from Arviat, the Elders made the following points:

> ICT will be used as a tool to enhance our role as socially responsible community members; ICT will be used to support the overall learning experience, and not as a means of replacing the acquisition of knowledge and skill through experience, but to support the overall learning experience; technology is good..., but it cannot replace experiential knowledge; traditional activities require a great deal of experience; ICT will serve to build collaborative relationships in a spirit of cooperation; ICT will be used to encourage creative problem solving and innovative thinking in order for the learner to pursue his/her full potential; a process not a finality. (IT Elders meeting, 2002)

The situation in Nova Scotia is very different. Although it is similar to Nunavut in that the government has placed a high priority on access to ICT, the penetration rates of high-speed Internet access and use are very high. As stated previously, the province has undertaken an initiative to ensure that every Nova Scotian will have broadband access to the Internet. "The goal is to make the province the most connected in all of North America" (Nova Scotia 2007). According to Statistics Canada's Canadian Internet Use Survey for 2005, in Nova Scotia, 67% of adults aged eighteen and over used the

Internet in the year prior to the survey for personal, non-business reasons. The Halifax figure was 75%, significantly higher than the 62% in the rest of the province (Statistics Canada 2006).

Although Nova Scotia communities are nowhere near as remote from each other, or as small as communities in Nunavut, the rural population makes up an important component of Nova Scotia's population. In 2001, rural and small-town residents comprised 36.7% of the total Nova Scotia population, a larger share of the provincial population than was the case Canada-wide (20.6%) (Rural Secretariat 2005).

In contrast to Nunavut, which is 85% Inuit, Nova Scotia is predominantly White, of European background (especially the British Isles and France). In 2001, less than 4% of those living in Nova Scotia had visible minority status (this compares to 13% in Canada as a whole). Many of these Nova Scotians were African Canadians, most of them Canadian-born.[6] Indeed, Halifax has the highest proportion of African Canadians of any major urban area in Canada, according to the 2001 census. Black residents account for 4% of the total population of Halifax and 52% of its visible minority population. First Nations groups make up a small minority of the Nova Scotia population (less than 2%; less than 1% in Halifax).

Unlike Nunavut, which has a few small communities separated by vast distances, Nova Scotia has numerous small communities, so that the outer edge of the province is almost continuously populated. Nevertheless, given limited public transportation and the relatively high rural population, distance and communication across that distance are still challenges. Despite the initiatives mentioned above, at the time the data collections were undertaken for the Equity and Technology project, many areas in rural Nova Scotia had no access to high-speed Internet.

So, why Nova Scotia and Nunavut? What can others learn from analyses from these two regions of Canada? Our original interest was in how ICT served various marginalized populations. Since it was beyond the scope of the project to do a nationally representative study (that being best left to Statistics Canada and other government agencies) a geographic focus was necessary. Rather than focusing on the typical, we opted to focus on those on the margins in various ways, with the understanding that marginal groups can provide numerous insights into both their own actions and, by contrast, those of the majority. Given our focus on *equity* in the study of technology among youth, it is perhaps more important to ensure that those already disadvantaged in some ways are not further disadvantaged by the increasing emphasis on ICT. Ideally, ICT could be used to mitigate some of the challenges facing various groups of young people in Canada.

Situated in the high Arctic, with a high concentration of Inuit, Nunavut is clearly on the "margins" of Canada, geographically and culturally. The challenge in this region that is of increasing strategic importance is maintaining connections with mainstream southern Canada without sacrificing the commitment to traditional Inuit culture. In different ways, Nova Scotia is also marginal; economically it has for some time been viewed as a "have-not" province. With its relatively high concentrations of African Canadians and its high rural population this Maritime province allows us to explore patterns of ICT access among these important subgroups of the Canadian population.

DATA COLLECTION

Most of the data collection was undertaken in the 2004–2005 academic year. Some carried over into the fall of 2005. Surveys were conducted with high school students and their teachers in Nova Scotia and Nunavut, with students in two NS alternative schools, with students in schools/faculties of education in Nova Scotia.[7] Interviews and focus groups were also undertaken with selected teachers in the high schools, faculty in the schools/faculties of education, a sample of street youth, and street youth organizations in urban Nova Scotia.[8] The high school surveys were designed and administered by Looker and Thiessen. Frank was responsible for the research with the schools/faculties of education, while Karabanow oversaw the work with the youth organizations.

The schools for the surveys were chosen in consultation with the participating departments of education. In Nova Scotia, given our interest in minority racial and ethnic groups, we wanted schools with high concentrations of African Canadians, and we chose a First Nations band-operated school. We chose schools in rural as well as urban areas, balancing large and small schools as best we could. In Nunavut we wanted to ensure that the three school districts were all represented, and we contacted the head offices in each district to get recommendations for schools in large as well as smaller communities. The implication of this process is that the schools are not representative in any formal way. Rather, this is a purposive sample.

The final sample includes ten[9] schools from Nova Scotia (including one band school), and thirteen from Nunavut (three in the Kitikmeot region, three in the Kivalliq, and seven in the Qikiqtani). In Nunavut the secondary schools include grade nine, so covered in the survey were grades nine to twelve in Nunavut, and grades ten to twelve in Nova Scotia.

Students under the age of eighteen had to obtain parental consent to participate in the survey in addition to giving their own consent. In Nunavut copies of the survey were made available in Inuktitut and Innuinaqtun; however, not one student completed the survey in either of these languages, responding instead in English. This fact may reflect differences in dialects that were not captured appropriately in the translations, or it may have more to do with the fact that while many of them speak their native tongue they have more experience writing in English. Nevertheless, the fact remains that many of these students were responding to the survey in their second language.[10]

All teachers in the participating schools were invited to complete a teacher survey; 119 completed it in Nova Scotia and sixty-one did in Nunavut. Also, twenty-two interviews were performed with teachers, administrators, and technical coordinators in the schools.

Two youth organizations were partners in the Research Alliance. Staff in these organizations participated in the focus groups and interviews. Interviews and focus groups were also undertaken with street youth.

All schools/faculties of education in Nova Scotia were invited to participate in the research. This involved having those students in the second year of their Bachelor of Education program who were preparing to be secondary school teachers complete a survey. There were also interviews and focus groups with faculty in these schools/faculties.

Table 1.1 presents an overview of the sample characteristics to set the stage for these analyses.

Table 1.1 shows the sample size and gender distribution for the different surveys that were undertaken. Overall, there are surveys from 2,527 high school students, 180 high school teachers, 139 students in the schools/faculties of education and twenty street youth. The gender split is fairly even, except for the fact that there are more female respondents in the sample from the schools/faculties of education (reflecting the female dominance of this subject area) and more males among the small sample of street youth. In the latter case, the surveys were designed to give a context for the more qualitative analyses that were undertaken with these youth.

Table 1.2 gives a more detailed breakdown of the high school respondents who form the basis for many of the survey analyses that follow. There are twice as many students from urban areas than there are from rural areas in

TABLE 1.1

Survey respondents by gender

	N	Male (%)	Female (%)
Nova Scotia students	1944	45	55
Nunavut students	583	51	49
Nova Scotia teachers	119	51	49
Nunavut teachers	61	51	49
Education students	139	32	68
Street youth	20	70	30

TABLE 1.2

High school student respondent characteristics

	Nova Scotia (%)	Nunavut (%)
Rural	33	53
Urban	67	47
Inuit	n/a	88
First Nations	8	2
African Canadian	8	1
White	75	8
Other	10	1
Grade 9	n/a	32
Grade 10	38	34
Grade 11	30	19
Grade 12	32	15

Nova Scotia, reflecting the pattern for the province as a whole. The pattern is different in Nunavut, and, given the small size of the communities there, we had to use a different operational definition. The capital, Iqaluit, has a total population of just over six thousand, according to the 2006 census (the closest census to our data collection); this community alone accounts for 21% of the total population of about thirty thousand. Added to this is the issue that there is just one high school in Iqaluit, so if Iqaluit were the only community counted as urban, any rural–urban comparisons in Nunavut would be identifying the specific school. In order to handle this issue, we classified two other communities as urban in light of the fact that they have a bank and daily jet service.[11] With this definition, 53% of our survey sample of Nunavut students live in rural areas.

Not surprisingly, there is more homogeneity in cultural background in Nunavut than in Nova Scotia; almost 90% of the student respondents there are Inuit. In Nova Scotia, the largest group is made up of the culturally dominant Whites, at 75%. As indicated above, our sample was designed to oversample members of the Mi'kmaq and African Canadian communities. They (and the residual category "other") each make up 8–10% of the student respondents.

As indicated above, the different grade distributions in the two research sites reflect the fact that high school includes grade nine in Nunavut, but not in Nova Scotia. The lower response rates in Nunavut in the higher grades parallels the patterns of grade retention, with dropout rates increasing as age increases.

Finally, Table 1.3 gives some highlights of the characteristics of the high school teachers who completed the survey. The rural–urban breakdown to some extent reflects the pattern of student respondents, although the difference in Nunavut is more pronounced. This result may reflect the fact that there were other events happening in the largest urban school the day the surveys were administered, so the teacher surveys were distributed later, when the researcher overseeing the process had left. The concentration of younger, less experienced teachers in the Nunavut sample is an indication of the extent to which recent graduates go to Nunavut from southern Canada for a few years but rarely stay for long.

TABLE 1.3

Teacher respondent characteristics

	Nova Scotia (%)	Nunavut (%)
Teach at rural school	42	53
Teach at urban school	58	47
Under 35 years old	30	88
36–45 years old	22	2
46–55 years old	34	1
56 years and over	14	1
Under 10 years teaching	34	32
11–20 years teaching	20	34
21 years teaching and over	46	23

Many of the analyses presented in this book involve analyses of data from the surveys. Details of how specific measures were coded, recoded and combined are included in the individual chapters.

DATA STRENGTHS AND LIMITATIONS

One of the key strengths of the data collection reflects the inclusion of rarely surveyed groups. Although there are a number of studies of the North; indeed it is often described as an "over-researched" area (Henderson 2007), it is rare to have research that compares both a northern territory and southern respondents. Similarly, having data with large enough sub-samples to compare African Canadians and First Nations youth to the dominant White European group is an asset. Having data from street youth and organizations that work with them is even more unusual. We have data from faculty and students in schools/faculties of education as well as teachers in high schools.

Further, we have quantitative survey data, and qualitative data from interviews, focus groups, and personal observation. We worked closely with the participating organizations whose members had input into the research design, the questions asked, and the interpretation of the results. All these characteristics strengthen the research results.

Some of these strengths come with tradeoffs, however. In order to ensure that our samples of the racial/ethnic subgroups were representative, we had to strategically sample schools, rather than trying to obtain a sample that was representative of the area. Given the available resources, the sample is restricted to two areas of Canada; larger more nationally representative samples must be left to organizations such as Statistics Canada. We discovered that it was difficult if not impossible to calculate response rates, especially in Nunavut, where the list of students attending the school at a given time is problematic for a number of reasons. These include the fact that students go by different names at times (minimally an English as well as an Inuit name) with different spellings, while at the same time several students have the same name. In addition, some students are absent from school for some time and then return, while others have effectively dropped out—but it is difficult to tell the difference at a given time. In other words calculating the population eligible for inclusion in the survey is problematic.

Our limited sample of First Nations youth is almost exclusively drawn from one band-operated school in a rural community. Almost all of the African Canadian youth are from urban schools in Halifax despite efforts to encourage

African Canadians in rural schools to participate. In other words, some of the results are limited in the extent to which they can be generalized to others, such as rural African Canadian students, off-reserve First Nations youth or youth belonging to First Nations groups other than the Mi'kmaq.

Another limitation, of course, is one we share with other researchers studying new technologies: the data are in some ways outdated before one even finishes collecting them. For example, the patterns in Nunavut are undoubtedly affected by the fact that, at the time of survey, there were no high-speed Internet connections in any community other than the capital, Iqaluit (and even that was slow by southern standards). The year following our data collections in Nunavut high-speed Internet was made available throughout the territory.[12] New modes of access to ICT, using cell phones, iPods, and personal digital assistants have no doubt proliferated in Nova Scotia as elsewhere in Canada since the time of this survey. While these changes will no doubt have an impact on the use of ICT by youth and others, they do not lessen the importance of having careful analyses of data at a given time, such as the analyses presented in this book.

OUTLINE OF THE BOOK

The next chapter, "Digital Distance," by Looker, examines the ongoing impact of geographic location on ICT access and use. Specifically it compares this access and use in rural versus urban locations and North–South differences in Canada by comparing results from Nova Scotia and Nunavut. This discussion sets the stage for an examination of other differences, including those based on culture and on gender, which are examined in detail in other chapters. A key issue in Looker's analysis is that, despite assurances that access is essentially ubiquitous for Canadian youth, there are still important differences in access and challenges created by those differences. The findings document that distance and context matter—for rural versus urban youth in both Nunavut and Nova Scotia and for those living in one of Canada's northern territories versus those in a more populous southern province. Access in the home to both computers and to high-speed Internet service reflects these different locations. Use, at school and at home, as well as skill development with ICT, is correspondingly patterned by geography and culture.

These cultural differences are explored in more detail in chapter 3, by Thiessen and Looker. Here the focus is on *effective* access and on how ICT is used to develop and strengthen social capital. The analysis also examines student attitudes to different learning media, and the implications of reliance on ICT for different cultural groups. As the authors show, there are small but significant differences not only in access to ICT but also in use, dispositions toward ICT, and skill development. There is some indication of resistance to the English-dominated world of computers and the Internet among some minority groups. Nevertheless, ICT is used as a medium for communicating with members of one's own group and (for some) for obtaining information about their culture and about others.

After reviewing some of the extensive literature on gender and the digital divide, Campbell and Hemming, in chapter 4, examine gender differences in attitudes toward and use of ICT among students in Nova Scotia and Nunavut. Analyses are done separately for the two sample areas, since, as Looker's chapter shows, north–south differences are huge. By looking in more detail at how and for what purpose ICT is used, Campbell and Hemming document how nuanced the gender differences are. While there is "male advantage" in some areas, there is female advantage in others—depending on whether one is looking at gaming, communication, self-reported skill levels, or perceived competencies. The authors then show the relationship between various ICT skills and academic performance in the two regions. They find not a simple digital divide, but rather digital *diversity* based on gender, a theme echoed throughout the book. What is more, there is evidence of what Campbell and Hemming call "digital distraction," where, for young women but not young men, high ICT use is correlated with lower academic performance. These and other findings show that the issue of gender differences with respect to ICT continues to warrant research attention.

In chapter 5, Naylor and Frank focus on the impact of technology on teachers by examining information from faculty and student teachers in schools/faculties of education. This chapter gets at the heart of the interaction between ICT and schooling by analyzing the effect of technology on equity in the classroom and the role of ICT on the development of social capital among student teachers and the faculty who teach them. The authors start by presenting evidence of the lack of conformity across schools regarding physical access to computers and the Internet, with more recently constructed schools having much more ICT equipment than older schools. This variation creates challenges for teachers in the schools as well as for teachers in training who work in different schools during their practicum training. This analysis also argues that there is a lack of effective integration of ICT into the curriculum in the faculties of education. As a result, student teachers often feel ill prepared to integrate it into the curriculum they will be implementing as teachers. It is clear that access does not automatically lead to the kind of literacy with ICT that proponents often champion. Rather, there is a need to focus on the set of practices with respect to ICT that are involved not only in teaching but in preparing future teachers. Without a clear identification of core ICT competencies that are necessary for future teachers, faculties of education provide few guidelines on how to use this technology to facilitate equity in the classroom. Clearly there is a need for more of a debate and discussion about the role of ICT in education, at the secondary and post-secondary level.

Chapter 6, by Looker and Naylor, continues the examination of equity and technology in education, shifting the focus from teachers in training to include teachers currently in secondary schools. The authors start with a recognition that there is little evidence of the "deep integration" across the curriculum foreseen by promoters of ICT in schools. Rather, classroom use tends to be on using ICT for relatively routine tasks: word processing, record keeping, and presentations, perhaps using information garnered online. Innovative and/or multi-media uses are rare. Much of the existing literature points to teacher attitudes and skills as key barriers to fuller integration of ICT into the curriculum. The findings in this chapter challenge that interpretation. Based on surveys of secondary school teachers, and of the student teachers discussed in chapter 5, Looker and Naylor report consistently positive attitudes of both groups to this technology. Further, both groups report relatively high levels of comfort with and skills in using ICT. There is little evidence of resistance here. One suggestion is that a range of curricular and organizational supports may be important to removing current barriers. Further, the results question the underlying assumption that ICT integration is limited or flawed if it has failed to transform pedagogical practices.

The final chapter, by Karabanow and Naylor, provides an interesting counterpoint to the other analyses in this book. While the other chapters discuss at some length the gaps and barriers and often nuanced differences in the use of ICT, this last chapter documents how one group of youth, street youth, use ICT in surprising ways. In this way the chapter expands both the research on street youth and research on ICT. Recent research on street youth recognizes both the dangers that young people are attempting to escape by living on the street as well as the dangers inherent in street life itself. After reviewing some key conceptual and empirical discussions of street youth, the authors discuss ICT within the complex context of street life, highlighting the parallels and differences between these youth and other "mainstream" young people. Based on in-depth qualitative interviews with twenty street youth, the authors detail some of the ways in which ICT help these youth feel connected to their social networks. The rather surprisingly high levels of use of ICT and the youths' reported high comfort levels with computers and the Internet allow them safe, asynchronous ways of communicating with friends and family. Further, computers, computer games, and the Internet offer street youth a way to safely pass time and "stay out of trouble." Nevertheless, given the realities of street life, it is important to recognize the challenges of ensuring that these already severely marginalized youth are not further marginalized by the increasing emphasis on ICT literacy in today's so-called knowledge economy.

In sum the chapters in this book can be seen to both complement and extend the existing literature on digital equity issues. They provide insight into some rarely researched groups—including ICT use in the high Arctic and among street youth. They include data not only on youth but also on their teachers and the faculty who are preparing future teachers. They look not only at digital divides but also at various forms of digital diversity. Finally, this book challenges some of our taken-for-granted assumptions about the ways that ICT can and are being used to facilitate equity for Canadian youth.

AUDIENCES

We see this book as being of interest and relevance to a number of audiences, including academics, policy-makers, and a range of educational and youth practitioners, as well as those members of the public (including young people themselves) interested in equity issues with respect to information and communication technology. In academia, those for whom these analyses would be relevant include sociologists in the areas of youth and/or in technology and education; those interested in cultural studies, gender issues, and northern studies; and social work faculty. Several of the chapters are germane to those in faculties of education and in departments specializing in the study of computers and society. Government service providers, especially those responsible for overseeing the provision of computers and related technology in schools and members of school boards will find several sections pertinent to their interests, as will government policy-makers and policy advocates. Practitioners who work with youth from various marginalized populations will find some of the results noteworthy. Finally, we hope the work will be interesting and informative for a variety of young people as they try to make sense of the role of ICT in their own lives.

NOTES

1   We would like to acknowledge and express our appreciation for the funding for this research project that was provided by the Social Sciences and Humanities Research Council of Canada under its Initiative on the New Economy. Note that the contributors to this book were not all members of the original research team; Campbell joined as collaborator assisting with the machine readable surveys and doing the gender analysis; Naylor was hired as Project Manager and gradually took over more responsibilities as co-author and co-editor. Alexander, who was on the research team, does not have an analysis in this book.

2   Some scholars also distinguish "linking" social capital—which involves bridging with others at a different position in a social hierarchy. We do not feel this additional distinction adds to our discussion of bridging and bonding social capital.

3   Updates are online at http://www.gov.ns.ca/econ/broadband/updates/.

4   These include income (OECD 2001; Reddick and Boucher 2002; Reddick, Boucher, and Groseilliers 2000; Rideout 2000); parental education (Corbett and Willms 2002; OECD 2001; Reddick, Boucher, and Groseilliers 2000; Rideout 2000); gender (Bimber 2000; Chinn and Fairlie 2007; Corbett and Willms 2002; Looker and Thiessen 2003; Looker 2007; OECD 2001; Reddick and Boucher 2002; Reddick, Boucher, and Groseilliers 2000; Rideout 2000); ethnicity (OECD 2001); immigration status (Corbett 2002); age (OECD 2001, Reddick et al. 2000; Rideout 2001); family structure and size (Corbett 2002); disability (OECD 2001; Rideout 2001); rural versus urban location (Rideout 2001; Looker and Thiessen 2003), and Aboriginal status (Rideout 2000; Thiessen and Looker 2008).

5   High-speed broadband connections were not available in Nunavut outside the capital, Iqaluit, until 2005, after the data analyzed in this book were collected.

6   According to the 2001 census, 91% of Halifax Blacks were born in Canada; their experiences with ICT will therefore reflect their experiences in Canada. While not all those who classify themselves as "Black" or of "African Heritage" are "African Canadians" (i.e., may or may not consider themselves Canadian), given the characteristics of our sample, we use the terms interchangeably.

7   While there are teacher education programs offered in Nunavut by the Nunavut Arctic College, these target students preparing to teach elementary schools. The focus of the research was on secondary school students and their current (and future) teachers so these Arctic College programs were not included in the data collections.

8   There were no equivalent youth organizations in Nunavut nor in rural Nova Scotia.

9   This number includes two urban schools, which were added in order to increase the number of African Canadian students, since the participation of these students in the surveys from rural schools was very low.

10   Other challenges faced conducting research in the Arctic are discussed in Looker, Thiessen, and Butler, 2006.

11 This suggestion was made by a member of the Nunavut Department of Education.
12 Interestingly Nova Scotia has yet to achieve access to high-speed Internet in all regions as of 2008; however, improvements to coverage and infrastructure continue to be made in 2010 and beyond (http://www.nunavut-broadband.ca/movingForward.htm).

WORKS CITED

Alkalimat, A. and K. Williams. 2001. *Social capital and cyberpower in the African American community.* In L. Keeble and B. Loader (eds.), *Community Informatics: Shaping Computer-mediated Social Relations,* 177–204. London: Routledge. http://www.communitytechnology.org/cyberpower.

Angrist, Joshua and Victor Lavy. 2002. "New Evidence on Classroom Computers and Pupil Learning." *The Economic Journal* 112(482): 735–65.

Attewell, P. 2001. "The First and Second Digital Divides." *Sociology of Education* 74:252–59.

Bezanson, Kate. 2006. "Gender and the Limits of Social Capital." *Canadian Review of Sociology and Anthropology* 43:427–43.

Bimber, B. 2000. " Measuring the Gender Gap on the Internet." *Social Science Quarterly* 81:868–76.

Bourdieu, Pierre. 1986. "The Forms of Capital." In *Handbook of Theory and Research for the Sociology of Education,* ed. J. Richardson, 241–58. New York: Greenwood Press.

Braverman, H. 1974. *Labor and Monopoly Capital.* New York: Monthly Review Press.

Cairncross, Frances. 1997. *The Death of Distance.* Boston: Harvard Business School Press.

Castells, Manuel. 1996. *The Rise of the Network Society, The Information Age: Economy, Society and Culture,* Vol. I. Oxford, UK: Blackwell (second edition, 2000).

Chinn, M.D. and R.W. Fairlie. 2007. "The Determinants of the Global Digital Divide: A Cross-country Analysis of Computer and Internet Penetration." *Oxford Economic Papers* 59:16–44.

Coleman, J.S. 1988. "Social Capital in the Creation of Human Capital." *American Journal of Sociology* 94:S95–S120.

Conrad, David. 2007. "Defining Social Capital." *Electronic Journal of Sociology.*

Corbett, B.A. and D.J. Willms. 2002. "Information and Communication Technology: Access and Use." *Education Quarterly Review* 8:11–12.

Cuban, Larry. 2001. *Oversold and Underused: Computers in the Classroom.* Cambridge, MA: Harvard University Press.

Cuneo, C. 2002. "Globalized and Localized Digital Divides along the Information Highway: A Fragile Synthesis across Bridges, Ramps, Cloverleaves, and Ladders." 33rd Annual Sorokin Lecture, University of Saskatchewan, Saskatoon, Canada. 30 January.

Dale, Ann and Ted Naylor. 2005. "Dialogue and Public Space: An Exploration of Radio and Information Communications Technologies." *Canadian Journal of Political Science* 38:203–25.

Daniel, Ben, Richard A. Schweir, and Gordon McCalla. 2003. "Social Capital in Virtual Learning Communities and Distributed Communities of Practice." *Canadian Journal of Learning and Technology*, vol. 29(3). http://www.cjlt.ca/content/vol29.3/cjlt29-3art7.html.

Downing, R. 2002. "Bridging Aboriginal Digital and Learning Divides." HRSDC, Office of Learning Technologies (OLT). Ottawa. http://www.hrsdc.gc.ca/en/hip/lld/olt/Skills_Development/OLTResearch/bridging-aboriginal-divide_e.pdf.

Dutta-Bergman, Mohan J. 2005. "Access to the Internet in the Context of Community Participation and Community Satisfaction." *New Media and Society* 7:89–109.

Fuchs, Thomas and Ludgar Woessman. 2004. "Computers and Student Learning: Bivariate and Multivariate Evidence on the Availability and Use of Computers at Home and at School." *Brussels Economic Review* 47(3–4): 359–85.

Gaved, Mark and Ben Anderson. 2006. "The Impact of Local ICT Initiatives on Social Capital and Quality of Life." Colchester: University of Essex, Chimera Working Paper 2006-6.

Gewirtz, S. and S. Ball. 2000. "From 'Welfarism' to 'New Managerialism': Shifting Discourses of School Headship in the Education Marketplace." *Discourse*. 21(3): 253–68.

Halpern, D. 2005. *Social Captial*. Cambridge: Polity Press.

Henderson, Ailsa. 2007. *Nunavut: Rethinking Political Culture*. Vancouver: University of British Columbia Press.

Keyway, J., E. Bullen, and S. Robb. 2004. "The Knowledge Economy, the Technopreneur and the Problematic Future of the University." *Policy Futures in Education* 2(2): 330–49.

Kim, D., S.V. Subramanian, and I. Kawachi. 2006. "Bonding versus Bridging Social Capital and Their Associations with Self Rated Health: A Multilevel Analysis of 40 US Communities." *Journal of Epidemiology and Community Health* 60:116–22.

Krahn, H. 1997. "On the Permanence of Human Capital: Use It or Lose It." *Public Policy Options* 18:17–21.

Krishna, A. 2001. "Moving from the Stock of Social Capital to the Flow of Benefits: The Role of Agency." *World Development* 29:925–43.

Leonard, Madeleine. 2004. "Bonding and Bridging Social Capital: Reflections from Belfast." *Sociology* 38:927–44.

Lin, Nan. 2000. "Inequality in Social Capital." *Contemporary Sociology* 29:785–95.

Looker, E.D. 2003. Teaching and Learning Technology: Enhancing Equity for Canadian Youth. SSHRC-INE Application. Ottawa.

———. 2007. "Gender and Information and Communication Technology (IT)." In *International Handbook of Information Technology in Education.* New York: Springer.

Looker, E.D. and V. Thiessen. 2002. "Digital Divide in Canadian Schools: Factors Affecting Student Access to and Use of Information Technology." Statistics Canada and Council of Ministers of Education. http://dsp-psd.pwgsc.gc.ca/Collection/Statcan/81-597-X/81-597-XIE.pdf.

———. 2003. "Beyond the Digital Divide in Canadian Schools: From Access to Competency in the Use of Information Technology." *Social Science Computer Review* 21:475–90.

Lloyd, C. and Jonathan Payne. 2003. "The Political Economy of Skill and the Limits of Educational Policy." *Journal of Education Policy* 18(1): 85–107.

Milton, P. 2003. Trends in the Integration of ICT and Learning in K–12 Systems. http://www.cea-ace.ca/media/en/Trends_ICT_Integration.pdf.

Narayan, Deepa. 1999. "Bonds and Bridges: Social Capital and Poverty." World Bank. Policy Research Working Paper No. 2167. http://www.psigeorgia.org/pregp/files/social%20capital.pdf.

Natriello, G. 2001. "Bridging the Second Digital Divide: What Can Sociologists of Education Contribute?" *Sociology of Education* 74: 260–65.

Nooteboom, Bart. 2007. "Social Capital, Institutions and Trust." *Review of Social Economy* LXV:29–53.

Norris, Pippa. 2003. "Social Capital and ICTs: Widening or Reinforcing Social Networks?" *International Forum on Social Capital for Economic Revival,* 1–29. Tokyo, Japan: Economic and Social Research Institute. http://www.esri.go.jp/en/workshop/030325/030325paper6-e.pdf.

Nova Scotia. 2007. Broadband for Rural Nova Scotia. http://www.gov.ns.ca/econ/broadband/.

OECD. 1996. *The Knowledge-based Economy.* Paris. http://www.oecd.org/dataoecd/51/8/1913021.pdf.

———. 2001. "Bridging the Digital Divide: Issues and Policies in OECD Countries." Paris: Organization for Economic Cooperation and Development. Pub. No. JT00110878.

———. 2004. "Developing Highly Skilled Workers: Review of Canada." http://www.oecd.org/dataoecd/2/0/34457947.pdf.

Parayil, G. 2005. "The Digital Divide and Increasing Returns: Contradictions of Informational Capitalism." *The Information Society* 21:41–51.

Peters, A.M. 2003. "Education Policy in the Age of Knowledge Capitalism." *Policy Futures in Education* 1(2): 361–81.

Pigg, Kenneth E. and Laura Duffy Crank. 2004. "Building Community Social Capital: The Potential and Promise of Information and Communication Technologies." *Journal of Community Informatics* 1(1):58–73. http://ci-journal.net/index.php/ciej/article/view/184/132.

Plante, J. 2005. "Connectivity and ICT Integration in First Nations Schools: Results from the Information and Communications Technologies in Schools Survey, 2003/04." Ottawa: Statistics Canada. http://www.statcan.ca/bsolc/english/bsolc?catno=81-595-M2005034.

Plante, J. and D. Beattie, D. 2004. "Connectivity and ICT Integration in Canadian Elementary and Secondary Schools: First Results from the Information and Communications Technologies in Schools Survey, 2003–2004." Education, Skills and Learning – Research Papers. Ottawa: Statistics Canada, Culture, Tourism and the Centre for Education Statistics Division. http://www.statcan.gc.ca/pub/81-595-m/81-595-m2004017-eng.pdf.

Policy Research Institute. 2005. "Social Capital as a Public Policy Tool." Ottawa: Policy Research Initiative.

Putnam, R.D. 2000. *Bowling Alone*. New York: Simon and Schuster.

Reddick, Andrew and Christian Boucher. 2002. "Tracking the Dual Digital Divide." Ottawa: HRSDC.

Reddick, Andrew, Christian Boucher, and Manon Groseilliers. 2000. "The Dual Digital Divide: The Information Highway in Canada." Ottawa: HRSDC.

Rideout, V. 2000. "Public Access to the Internet and the Canadian Digital Divide." *Canadian Journal of Information* and Library Science 25:1–21.

Rural Secretariat. 2005. Rural Nova Scotia Profile: A Ten Year Census Analysis (1991–2001). Rural Secretariat. http://www.rural.gc.ca/research/profile/ns_e.pdf.

Schuller, Tom. 2007. "Reflections on the Use of Social Capital." *Review of Social Economy* 65(1):11–28.

Sciadas, G. 2002. "Unveiling the Digital Divide." Ottawa: Statistics Canada. http://www.statcan.gc.ca/pub/56f0004m/56f0004m2002007-eng.pdf.

Snyder, Ilana. 1998. *Beyond Page to Screen: Taking Literacy into the Electronic Era*. London: Routledge.

Statistics Canada. 2006. "Canadian Internet Use Survey." *The Daily*, 15 August. http://www.statcan.ca/Daily/English/060815/d060815b.htm.

Stoll, Clifford. 2000. *High-tech Heretic: Confessions of a Computer Contrarian*. New York: Anchor Books.

Thiessen, V. and E.D Looker. 2007. "Digital Divides and Capital Conversion." *Information, Communication and Society* 10:159–80.

———. 2008. "Cultural Centrality and Information and Communication Technology among Canadian Youth." *Canadian Journal of Sociology* 33(2):311–36.

van Staveren, Irene. 2003. "Beyond Social Capital in Poverty Research." *Journal of Economic Issues* 37:415–23.

Wellman, Barry. 2001. "Physical Place and Cyberplace: The Rise of Personalized Networking." *International Journal of Urban and Regional Research* 25:227–52.

Wellman, Barry, Janet Salaff, Dimitrina Dimitrova, Laura Garton, Milena Gulia, and Caroline Haythornthwaite. 1996. "Computer Networks as Social Networks:

Collaborative Work, Telework, and Virtual Community." *Annual Review of Sociology* 22(1): 213–38.

Wilson, Samuel M. and Leighton C. Peterson. 2002. "The Anthropology of Online Communities." *Annual Review of Anthropology* 31:449–67.

Zuboff, S. 1984. *In the Age of the Smart Machine*. New York: Basic Books.

Zwaagstra, Michael. 2008. *Computers in the Classroom: Technology Overboard?* Winnipeg, MB: Frontier Centre for Public Policy.

Chapter 2

Digital distance: Geographic and cultural divides in access and use of computers and the Internet

E. Dianne Looker

If there is one divide that Information and Communication Technology (ICT) is perhaps best designed to overcome it is that of geographic distance. By removing the constraint imposed by synchronous, place-based forms of communication, ICT allows linkages across space, facilitating communication with others and access to information. One might expect, then, that priority be given to ensuring access to these technologies for those potentially most disadvantaged by the barriers created by geographic distance, particularly those in rural and remote areas of Canada. One might also expect that individuals and groups in these remote areas would most actively lobby for and embrace these technologies. I suspect few readers will be surprised to learn that, contrary to these expectations, one finds instead the quintessential digital divide.

This chapter examines issues relating to this divide based on social and geographic location. In many ways this chapter is designed to set the stage for some of the other discussions in this book by documenting the effects of *both* social and physical location on the development of facility with these technologies.

The Organisation for Economic Co-operation and Development (OECD 2001a; OECD 2001b, 23) defines the digital divide as the gap between individuals and groups "with regard to both their opportunities to access information and communication technology (ICTs) and to their use of

the Internet for a wide variety of activities" (OECD 2001a, 8). Although policy-makers have focused greatly on creating an advantageous climate for growing the knowledge economy, they have concentrated considerably less on ways
to ensure the development of an equitable knowledge *society*. In broad terms,
a knowledge society centres around the social capabilities to identify, process,
transform, disseminate, and use information to build and apply knowledge
for human development (UNESCO 2005). Although issues of access to technology and connectivity infrastructure remain essential, it is also important
that we recognize that inclusive access does not end at being "connected."
Rather, inclusion and participation in the knowledge society are tied to social
processes that are dynamic and complex and that vary across different cultural and geographic contexts. This chapter examines the digital divide in
terms of urban compared to rural youth, and starts the discussion of how race
intersects with these divides digitally.

Documentation of the digital divide based on geographic location in
several countries indicates that those in rural and remote areas have the least
rather than the most access to these technologies that ostensibly are designed
to dissolve distance (OECD 2001b). This divide has been conceptualized in
a number of different ways. Reddick et al. (2000) talk about a "dual" digital
divide: that between users and non-users, but also differences within the group
of users in terms of the ways ICT is used. Attewell (2001) and Natriello (2001)
make similar distinctions. Sciadas (2003) argues that rather than thinking of
the "haves" and "have nots," it makes more sense to talk about those who "have
more" and those who "have less." Regardless of the definition used there is
considerable recognition that it is important to continue to monitor access and
use of ICT by different groups. A broader concern about a digital divide in
Canada and internationally (Canada 1997; Canada 2001a; Canada 2001b;
Industry Canada 1996; Industry Canada 2001; McMullen and Rohrbach
2003) has led to policies and research on the subject as it relates specifically
to rural areas (Thiessen and Looker 2006).

Some of these geographic divides are relatively well documented. It is
clear that in many areas rural communities have less access to the technology,
particularly in terms of high-speed connections to the Internet (CRTC 2006;
McKeown, Noce. and Czerny, 2007; U.S. Department of Commerce 1995;
1999; 2004). Rural households have fewer computers and are less likely to
have computers with an Internet connection (Thiessen and Looker 2006).
As Cairncross (2001) notes, the irony is that access to this technology is even

more critical to those in rural areas. Nor is rural location the only issue in these analyses. Race and culture often overlap with rural locale, given the unequal distribution of cultural groups within a country, and many in rural areas (as well as those in inner cities) tend to fall into the "have not" category when it comes to access to ICT (Compaine 2001).

Interestingly, despite the relatively consistent message that these divides continue to exist, some researchers display considerable optimism for the future. Mitchell (2001) claims that "In the longer term, ... digital technology should have a powerful equalizing effect by delivering services and opportunities to those who would otherwise be excluded by location or lack of mobility, and by creating products and services that can be shared widely at a low cost" (Mitchell 2001, 162; see Rideout 2000 for a contrary view that sees these divides as widening). Compaine (2001) assumes that with the rapid diffusion of the technologies the digital divide, or at least that based on geography, will simply fade away. Of course, Cairncross (2001, 290) is among the most optimistic. Her book *The Death of Distance* claims that not only will the grip of distance die but that the effect of this shift will be to narrow gaps, not widen them. She sees this technology bridging distance between not only rural and urban areas but also among cultural groups. Groups spread over a large distance will be able to maintain communication, and diverse groups can create links with others. In other words, technology can be used to create and strengthen both bridging and bonding social capital (Thiessen and Looker 2006). Clearly, however, it can create and strengthen these forms of social capital only if rural youth have access to the technology. Even Cairncross recognizes that "the death of distance loosens the grip of geography. It does not destroy it" (2001, 5). Regardless of whether one buys into this optimism, the challenge, according to Mitchell (2001, 162), is "to find ways of mitigating the short term problems while moving as rapidly as possible to achieve the long term benefits" of these technologies. In other words, there is recognition that a divide based on geography and ones based on culture still exist and are, in many cases, intertwined.

Those living in rural areas are, for all intents and purposes, *defined* by their physical location. Few other markers of identity or social location are as place based. Even nationality can become blurred given that, for example, Canadians living abroad are often still defined (by themselves and others) as Canadian. An individual from a rural area is rarely considered to still be rural if they move to an urban setting. What is more, rural *places* can lose their claim as they are amalgamated into urban municipalities and/or grow beyond a certain size. The *essence* of being rural is that you are physically in (or outside) a small community, distant[1] from an urban centre.

Assuming one wants to both maintain rural populations and ensure equitable access to resources and services across Canada, then the issue of rural access to ICT becomes important. As more government services are available online and more reliance is placed on distance education to service remote areas, access to high-speed connections becomes more and more critical in rural and remote parts of the country. Given the heavy reliance on private Internet providers, however, who understandably want to make a profit on their investments, sparsely populated rural areas are often the last served (Alter et al. 2007; Malecki 2003). This is unfortunate, since one can argue that the ones who most need access to these resources are those in rural areas who have limited or no access to other services and resources in their community (and often have limited access to public transportation to a larger centre). Indeed, some argue that rural and remote communities in Canada should be given assistance "in order to gain the access required to be full participants in the information society" (McKeown, Noce, and Czerny 2007, 4; see also Ferguson 2004 and Ramírez 2001). With close to a third of Canada's population living in rural areas, this digital divide warrants our careful attention.

This chapter provides detailed comparative data about youth access to and use of ICT in two regions of Canada that each have significant rural populations but with different patterns of population dispersion. After providing an overview of the data and measures used, the first analysis section examines youth in rural versus urban Nova Scotia. These youth are comparable in many ways to youth in the other southern Canadian provinces. It then examines the ways that the challenges facing youth in the northern territory of Nunavut differ from those facing youth in the south. Having comparable data from two disparate regions of Canada provides information and insights not otherwise possible. Finally, the chapter looks in some detail at these northern youth, comparing Inuit students, who comprise the majority, with the smaller group of non-Inuit living in the territory. As indicated above, one of the main goals of this chapter is to set the stage for some of the more nuanced analyses of *how* youth use ICT by documenting the more fundamental divides of access and time spent using ICT.

DATA AND METHODS

The data for this analysis come from the surveys conducted with the high school youth who are part of the Equity and Technology project, undertaken in 2004–2005. The survey asked a number of questions about the students' computer use, their home situation, and various attitudes about themselves, their school, and their future. In this analysis the main focus will be on three components of ICT use:

Access Measures include whether the student has access to a computer in their home, whether such a computer has Internet access and, if so, if the connection is high-speed or dial-up.

Use Students were asked how much time they spent last week on computers at home,[2] at school, at a friend's, in a public place. The original categories were recoded as follows: none = 0, less than 2 hours = 1, 2 to 5 hours = 3.5, 6 to 10 hours = 8, 11 to 15 hours = 13, 16 to 20 hours = 17.5, over 20 hours = 21. Total time was created from a sum of these, with this total capped at 40.

Skill One measure of skill used in this analysis involves a sum of nineteen self-report items. On a four-point scale (1 "I don't know how to do this," 2 "I can do this but sometimes I need help," 3 "I can do this without help," 4 "I can teach others to do this") students ranked their ability on a range of tasks from cutting and pasting to creating a web page. The second measure is based on their self-reported level of competence on a scale of 1 to 7, where 7 was coded as "expert."

The measure of rural versus urban location was more straightforward in Nova Scotia than in Nunavut. There are two urban areas in Nova Scotia: the Halifax-Dartmouth metropolitan region and Sydney; all other areas are considered rural.[3] In Nunavut we have included the capital, Iqaluit, plus Rankin Inlet and Cambridge Bay (which have a bank and daily jet service). As stated in chapter 1, 53% of the Nunavut respondents are rural and 47% urban; the corresponding percentages for Nova Scotia are 33% rural and 67% urban.

In the Nunavut part of the analysis, we want to identify not only those who self-identify as Inuit but also gauge their commitment to their traditional language and culture. Although the survey has only imperfect measures of this commitment, we do have information on their feelings about the language (Inuktitut or Inuinnaqtun) in terms of whether they would want their children to learn their mother tongue in addition whether or not they agree that one needs English to succeed. There is also a question on whether they want to stay in Nunavut. These measures, albeit limited, give an indication of commitment to the traditional way of life in Nunavut.

FINDINGS
Rural–urban divides in the south
First we look at the patterns for at the Nova Scotia youth, focusing on rural–urban differences. The key starting place is to consider whether these youth have similar access to technology in their homes.

As Table 2.1 clearly shows, the answer is "no." The two-thirds of Nova Scotia students who live in urban areas are more likely to have Internet access in their homes (93% versus 87% in rural areas).[4] There is an even larger difference in terms of those with high-speed access versus dial-up. Only 53% of rural respondents said they had high-speed Internet at home at the time of the survey (2004–2005); this compares to 86% of urban youth. This is a statistically significant difference with major implications. Teachers in some rural schools reported being reluctant to assign homework that required work on the web, given that not all their students could easily access it (personal communication with teacher, rural Nova Scotia). Indeed, one principal commented on how he could not do some of the preparatory work he'd like to do at home because, although he had high-speed Internet access at school, a few minutes' drive away at his home, it was not available (personal communication). In other words, this lack of home access has implications for the ways schools organize their work. The access is often restricted not by the unwillingness or inability of the family or household to subscribe to a high-speed Internet service but by the fact that it is not physically available.

Looking next at the time spent on computers, we find that it does not vary much by rural versus urban location in Nova Scotia. Both groups of youth spend, on average, about 13 hours per week on computers in some locale.

TABLE 2.1
Type of Internet connection at home by rural–urban location in Nova Scotia

Type of Connection	Urban	Rural
No Internet connection (%)	7	14
Dial-up only (%)	7	34
High-speed connection (%)	86	53
N	1155	601

Urban students spend slightly more time on computers at home (9.5 hours versus 8.8 hours), a small difference that does not reach statistical significance. However, rural youth spend somewhat more time at school (2.2 hours a week on average versus 1.5 hours for urban). Note how low these figures are, however. It is clear that school is not the place where most Nova Scotia youth spend their computer time. Nevertheless, this result is important since it does suggest that rural youth are able, to some extent, to counter the disadvantage of limited home access by spending more time using ICT in school. This finding is confirmed in the analysis of a national data set that shows the same pattern (Looker and Thiessen 2003).

The pattern of home use shifts if one looks at *type* of Internet connection in their home.[5] As Table 2.2 shows, the apparent rural–urban consistencies in time spent on computers mask some important differences. Not surprisingly, those with the lowest levels of use are those with no home Internet connection. More interesting is the fact that those who spend the most time on their home computers and the most time overall are *rural* students with high-speed access in their homes. Further, urban students with a dial-up connection spend less time using ICT than rural students with this type of connection. In other words, the rural–urban differences contain some important differences by type of connectivity. What is more, this finding suggests that there is no resistance on the part of rural youth to the technology. If they are given equal access, they use it as much or more than their urban counterparts. This result is consistent with our argument that ICT access has the potential to overcome some of the distance-based disadvantages faced by rural youth, in Nova Scotia and perhaps elsewhere.

TABLE 2.2

Average time spent on different computers by rural–urban location and type of connection in Nova Scotia

Mean time on ICT (hours per week)[a]	Urban high-speed	Rural high-speed	Urban dial-up	Rural dial-up	Urban no Internet	Rural no Internet
At home	10.7	11.1	6.4	7.9	1.0	1.6
At school	1.5	2.5	1.6	1.8	2.3	2.0
On public PCs	0.3	0.4	0.1	0.2	1.2	0.8
Total[a]	14.0	15.6	9.6	11.8	6.4	6.3

[a]Total time also includes time spent on a friend's computer.

TABLE 2.3

Average skill levels and self-reported competence, Nova Scotia, by rural–urban location and home connectivity

	Skills (1–4)	Competence (1–7)
Total urban	3.27	5.28
Total rural	3.15	5.21
High-speed urban	3.36	5.42
High-speed rural	3.32	5.15
Dial-up urban	3.14	5.42
Dial-up rural	3.06	4.63
No Internet urban	2.86	4.94
No Internet rural	2.83	4.67

In terms of skills, rural students, regardless of the type of connection, tend to have slightly lower reported skill levels. Overall, they score lower on the four-point scale (3.15 versus 3.27 for urban students; see Table 2.3). It is clear, however, that the largest differences are due not to rural versus urban location but rather to type of connectivity. The right-hand column of Table 2.3 shows a similar pattern for the youths' self-reported levels of competence. Although there are some urban–rural differences, always in favour of the urban youth, the main difference can be attributed to type of Internet connection in the home.

Taking this one step further, using multiple regression techniques (see Table 2.4) we see the impact of type of home connectivity and time spent on computers to both skill and reported levels of competence. The factors directly related to these measures of ICT ability are: type of connection and time spent on computers, with socio-economic status (as measured by maternal education) having some impact on skills and on reports of competence by gender (see Thiessen [2007] for an insightful analysis of self-reports by gender). There is no evidence of a direct effect of rural–urban location per se; however, rural versus urban location would have an effect via the type of connection available in their homes, and the time spent on computers (since we have seen that these differ by geographic locale).

In other words, the differences in material access to computers and to high-speed connections that persist in Nova Scotia have repercussions not only for the amount of time young people spend using ICT but also the range of ICT-related skills they develop and their feelings of competence with respect

TABLE 2.4

Multiple regression analysis of (a) computer skills and (b) self-reported competence, Nova Scotia

	Skills (1–4)		Competence (1–7)	
	β	Sig.	β	Sig.
Rural location	−.04	ns	.01	ns
Home connectivity	.20	***	.15	***
Total time spent on computers	.22	***	.25	***
Socio-economic status (mother's education)	.06	*	.02	ns
Female	−.03	ns	−.06	*
R^2	.12		.11	
N	1427		1426	

*** = sig. at .0001; ** = sig. at .01; * = sig. at .05; ns = not sig.

to this technology. These differences are likely to have implications for their experiences in school and beyond.

So, in the south (which is where the vast majority of Canada's population lives) rural–urban location continues to have an effect, but it is a difference driven mostly by the type of home access to computers and the Internet. As computer ownership and high-speed access become more ubiquitous, we might expect many of these differences to decrease if not disappear. Indeed there is the suggestion of a possible reversal of the rural–urban divide once more rural students have access to high-speed connections. An intriguing group is the urban students with a dial-up connection in their home. Is this a matter of consumer choice or a reflection of the higher costs associated with accessing high-speed connections? This question warrants further investigation.

North–south differences

One of the unique components of this research project is that there are comparable data from both a southern province and a northern territory. We have documented that even in the south there are important differences based on one's geographic location. Given the even greater dispersion of communities in Nunavut and the small size of these communities, the north–south differences are undoubtedly huge. These will be briefly highlighted before turning to a more detailed analysis of rural–urban differences in the north.

As can be seen in Table 2.5, those living in Nova Scotia are much more likely to have a computer in their home and much more likely to have an

TABLE 2.5

Home access to ICT by north–south and rural–urban location

Home access	Urban NU	Rural NU	Urban NS	Rural NS
No home computer (%)	23	57	4	6
Computer, no Internet (%)	17	21	2	6
One or more Internet connections (%)	61	22	94	88
N	265	296	1295	631

Internet connection than youth in Nunavut. Over half of the rural Nunavut respondents (57%) report having no computer in their home. This compares with 23% of those in urban Nunavut. However, the key comparison here is the fact that that less than 10% of Nova Scotia students say this, regardless of whether they live in rural or urban areas. Even the relatively high Internet access in urban Nunavut, at 61% (compared to 22% in rural Nunavut), is low when one looks at the figures for Nova Scotia, which are close to or over 90%. As indicated in chapter 1, Canada is positioned well relative to other countries in terms of providing access to computers; nevertheless, our results clearly indicate that this access is not shared by Canadians in all regions.

If we look more closely at access to high-speed Internet, which was not available to any extent in Nunavut at the time of the study,[6] the access divide becomes even more pronounced. It goes without saying that Nova Scotia students are more likely to have high-speed access. Only 1% of rural Nunavut youth say they have access to high-speed Internet service; 22% of urban Nunavut youth say the same. This compares to 53% and 86% in rural and urban Nova Scotia. This rural–urban difference within Nova Scotia is still much less than the north–south difference, however.

Although not large, there are similar north–south differences in time spent on computers, even in this ethnic subgroup. White students in Nova Scotia spend more time on the computer per week than their counterparts in Nunavut, most of it at home (data not shown). Interestingly, these youth in Nunavut spend slightly more time using public sites. However, these differences are relatively minor compared to those reflecting the differences between the Inuit population of Nunavut and their non-Inuit counterparts in the territory, an analysis to which we now turn.

In this brief overview we see a different sort of impact of distance and location on access and use of ICT. Certain areas of the country, in this case the far north, present a very different environment for young people. It is important to remember this fact when we boast of Canada's high levels of connectivity relative to other countries. There is still a deep digital divide, even in terms of physical access to the technology in Canada.

Rural–urban divides in the north

Any analyses in Nunavut have to take into account the fact that the majority of the population is Inuit and that the Inuit/non-Inuit populations are unevenly distributed in the urban versus the rural areas. Therefore any rural–urban comparisons in Nunavut should also consider the breakdown by race/culture.

Table 2.6 does this and shows there are still large rural–urban differences in access among the Inuit. There are not enough rural non-Inuit in the sample (N=15) to include these in the analysis; however, note that the rural–urban difference for the Inuit in Table 2.6 is almost identical to the overall rural–urban pattern evident in Table 2.5. It is the differences among the Inuit living in rural as compared to urban areas that is driving the overall difference, not so much the fact that there are differences in the ethnic composition in the two locales.[7]

There are a number of factors that could be affecting this access. One is the cost of ICT associated with living in a rural locale in Nunavut. Not all communities have their own Internet provider, meaning that access would require a long-distance telephone call. Given this, socio-economic status (SES) is likely an important determinant of access. The best measure of SES in the data set for Nunavut is whether the household has a digital camera.[8] Another issue is that rural–urban differences may reflect the fact that the Inuit in more

TABLE 2.6

Home access to ICT by rural–urban location and ethnicity in Nunavut

Home access	Urban non-Inuit	Urban Inuit	Rural Inuit
No home computer (%)	15	24	57
Computer, no Internet (%)	4	19	21
One or more Internet connections (%)	80	57	21
N	46	219	282

Note: There are too few non-Inuit in rural areas to include this category.

rural communities are more tied to their traditional lifestyles. The lack of access to ICT in their homes may reflect resistance on their part to this English-dominated technology "from the south." The data set provides a number of possible measures of adherence to the traditional Inuit lifestyle: whether they agree that they want to spend their life in Nunavut, their commitment to having their children know their traditional language, and whether or not they think one needs English to succeed.

We have already seen that there are significant differences in Nunavut between the Inuit majority and the non-Inuit minority (who are concentrated in the capital of Iqaluit). The interesting question, then, becomes what factors affect the levels of home access of the Nunavut students. Table 2.7 shows a multi-variate analysis of this access (whether one has a computer and if so how many have Internet connections) for all Nunavut respondents and then separately for the Inuit students.

First note that even after controlling on these other variables there is still a large and statistically significant effect of rural location on home access to this technology. This is true whether one considers all respondents or just those identified as Inuit. Being Inuit does have an impact; Inuit students report less access than their non-Inuit counterparts even after the other controls. Not surprisingly, those with higher SES have more

TABLE 2.7

Multiple regression analysis of home ICT access in Nunavut, all respondents and Inuit only

	All youth		Inuit	
	β	Sig.	β	Sig.
Rural location	−.25	***	−.23	***
Socio-economic status (digital camera)	.41	***	.42	***
Want children to learn traditional language	−.04	ns	−.01	ns
Wants to spend life in Nunavut	−.07	ns	−.08	ns
You need English to succeed	.08	ns	.09	*
Inuit	−.12	**		
R^2	.36		.31	
N	485		433	

*** = sig. at .0001; ** = sig. at .01; * = sig. at .05; ns = not sig.

ICT. In terms of cultural attitudes, there is little evidence of an effect, either in terms of embracing or resisting the technology. Neither wanting your children to learn one of the traditional Inuit languages nor wanting to stay in Nunavut has an impact on home access to this technology. The only suggestion of a relationship with cultural values is the fact that, for the Inuit respondents, feeling that one needs to learn English to succeed in Nunavut is associated with having more ICT access. However, for this analysis perhaps the important issue is that there is a still a rural–urban difference that cannot be accounted for by any of these variables. Location still matters.

Looking next at *use patterns* in the north, we again see some rural–urban differences. As we did in Table 2.6, we have included in Table 2.8 both rural–urban and Inuit/non-Inuit comparisons. Once more we see fairly large, rural–urban differences among the Inuit, particularly in the time spent on home computers and time spent overall. It is interesting that those in rural areas with relatively limited home access to ICT do not compensate more for this fact by using computers more at school, especially considering that we noted earlier that this type of compensation does seem to happen to some extent for rural Nova Scotia youth. In Nunavut the communities are very small, so there are no large distances involved in travel to school, no time constraints imposed by busing schedules, and the school computers are often available after school hours. It is not clear why those who have limited home access do not use school facilities more. The only place this compensation seems to occur is for urban Inuit youth using public computers. Although the lower levels of use in rural areas may have to do with confidence and skills levels (factors we will examine below), this pattern suggests they do not seem to be simply culturally based.

TABLE 2.8

Hours spent using ICT by rural–urban location and ethnicity in Nunavut

Hours (per week spent on ICT)	Urban non-Inuit	Urban Inuit	Rural Inuit
At home	9.6	3.1	1.1
At school	2.0	1.8	1.2
On public PCs	0.4	1.1	0.5
Total[a]	13.9	7.2	3.4

Note: There are too few non-Inuit in rural areas to include this category.

[a]The "total" figures also include time spent on friends' computers.

TABLE 2.9

Multiple regression of total time spent on computers in Nunavut, all respondents and Inuit only

	All youth		Inuit	
	β	Sig.	β	Sig.
Rural location	−.13	**	−.13	**
Level of home ICT access	.20	***	.18	**
Socio-economic status (digital camera)	.10	*	.11	*
Want children to learn traditional language	−.07	ns	−.06	ns
Wants to spend life in Nunavut	−.12	**	−.12	**
You need English to succeed	.06	ns	−.06	ns
Inuit	−.12	**		
R^2	.22		.15	
N	485		433	

*** = sig. at .0001; ** = sig. at .01; * = sig. at .05; ns = not sig.

The largest difference in Table 2.8 is between non-Inuit and Inuit youth in urban areas. Here we do see some important cultural differences. Time spent on computers at home is much larger for urban non-Inuit than it is for Inuit respondents (9.6 for non-Inuit versus 3.1 for Inuit). Some of this difference undoubtedly reflects the differential access to ICT in their homes. However, as the multi-variate analysis above documents, this is not the whole story.

As in Table 2.7, we run two models in Table 2.9: one for all Nunavut respondents, the second restricted to Inuit respondents to show the impact of being Inuit on time spent using computers and the Internet. Home access obviously does have an effect, indeed the largest direct effect, in both models. As one might expect, the more home access, the more time one spends on computers. SES also has a separate direct effect on computer use, even with controls. Again we see that rural location has a direct effect as well as an indirect one via the home access measure. There is some suggestion of traditional values having an impact, as those who say they want to stay in Nunavut tend to spend less time on computers. However, the questions about language have no direct effect in either model.

The analysis for all Nunavut youth shows that being Inuit has a statistically significant impact on time spent on computers, even after taking into

TABLE 2.10

Mean skill levels by rural–urban location and ethnicity in Nunavut

Mean skill	Urban non-Inuit	Urban Inuit	Rural Inuit
On tasks (1–4)	3.0	2.4	1.9
Overall competence (1–7)	4.9	4.3	3.9
N	46	226	282

Note: There are too few non-Inuit in rural areas to include this category.

account direct access issues, by controlling on home access and SES. This point warrants further examination (which is undertaken in chapter 3). At this stage, perhaps the important point is to focus on the persistent effect of rural versus urban location, even in this northern territory, which is itself remote from the rest of Canada.

Finally we consider how the rural–urban divide influences the development of ICT-related skills. We have two measures, one (ranging from a low of 1 to a high of 4) is the average of the student's self-reported ability to do nineteen different tasks; the second is their self-reported level of competence, on a scale from 1 to 7 where 7 is "expert." Given that these are averages on relatively restricted scales, apparently minor differences are important.

Table 2.10 shows clearly that the non-Inuit in urban areas see themselves as more accomplished across a range of tasks than urban Inuit do, who in turn see themselves as more skilled than do rural Inuit. This pattern holds for both self-reported measures of skill and competence. The fact that rural Inuit rate their skills lowest of the three groups appears to be at variance with what McMullen and Rohrbach (2003) report for several remote Canadian Aboriginal communities. On the basis of a qualitative study, they report that Aboriginal students in remote communities are more comfortable with technology than students who live close to urban centres.

The corresponding multi-variate analysis (Table 2.11) confirms that, not surprisingly, both home access and time spent on computers contribute to higher levels of self-reported skill. It also shows that both rural location and being Inuit have direct effects on skill development. Adherence to a traditional Inuit lifestyle has little or no direct effect here. Indeed, the fact that those who say one needs English to succeed report higher skill levels suggests that embracing this technology is part of a package of adapting to it being an English-dominated medium. SES has no effect on skills once home access to ICT and the other control variables are taken into account.

TABLE 2.11

Multiple regression of self-reported computer skills in Nunavut, all respondents and Inuit only

	All youth		Inuit	
	β	Sig.	β	Sig.
Rural location	−.17	***	−.19	***
Level of home ICT access	.26	***	.26	***
Hours using computers	.28	***	.29	***
Socio-economic status (digital camera)	.05	ns	.05	ns
Want children to learn traditional language	.00	ns	.04	ns
Wants to spend life in Nunavut	−.08	*	−.08	ns
One needs English to succeed	.13	***	.14	**
Inuit	−.11	**		
R^2	.44		.36	
N	484		433	

*** = sig. at .0001; ** = sig. at .01; * = sig. at .05; ns = not sig.

We have a picture now that shows not only that access and time on computers affect skill development, but also that rural students report lower levels of skills independent of these access issues. Further, Inuit students report lower skill levels. The lack of impact of the measures of adherence to traditional life styles suggests that the issue may be less one of active resistance than it is lack of exposure to the skills. The question remains why Inuit students and those in rural schools would have lower exposure to the necessary skills.

The final analysis looks at a similar issue—the youths' self-reported competence. This measure is even more subjective than the skills one (which involves asking how well they feel they can do nineteen specific tasks). With these results, the picture is somewhat different. We see no direct relationship with either rural location or with being Inuit. In other words, despite the differential reports of skill levels, Inuit students are no less confident in their ICT competence than non-Inuit. Rural students are no less confident than urban. This finding suggests that their reference points are students in their own schools and others in their own community.

For this analysis the critical point is that rural location has an apparent impact on skills development for all Nunavut youth, and for the Inuit

TABLE 2.12

Multiple regression of self-reported competence with ICT in Nunavut, all respondents and Inuit only

	All youth		Inuit	
	β	Sig.	β	Sig.
Rural location	.05	ns	.04	ns
Level of home ICT access	.19	***	.17	**
Hours using computers	.27	***	.23	***
Socio-economic status (digital camera)	.02	ns	.01	ns
Want children to learn traditional language	.12	*	.14	**
Wants to spend life in Nunavut	−.05	ns	−.05	ns
One needs English to succeed	.14	**	.13	**
Inuit	−.08	ns		
R^2	.18		.14	
N	480		429	

*** = sig. at .0001; ** = sig. at .01; * = sig. at .05; ns = not sig.

majority, but not on levels of self-confidence with the technology. Of course, reported skills are related to confidence levels (data not shown), but this does not take away from the importance of the patterns reported here.

Despite this last finding about levels of reported competence, overall we see that within Nunavut there are some clear and consistent differences based on location. It is not just geographic location that matters, however. Cultural location has its own impact. The patterns of access, use, and skill development differ between the Inuit and non-Inuit, even within the urban settings. The underlying factors are complex, but we can conclude that both social and geographic contexts matter.

DISCUSSION AND CONCLUSION

What can we conclude from these results? It is clear there are still differences in access, use, and skill development based on rural versus urban location, and these differences are even more pronounced in the far north. Not all of the differences point to a rural disadvantage, however. In some cases, rural youth (e.g., rural youth in Nova Scotia with access to high-speed connections in their homes) use computers more than others.

Issues related to access are fairly clear and could be called a "digital divide," where there are "haves" and "have nots" (or those who have more versus those who have less). Rural youth in the north, indeed all those living in the far north, appear to have less access to the technology and to affordable and high-speed Internet access. Both Inuit and non-Inuit youth in the north have very different patterns of access than their counterparts in the south. Some areas of rural Nova Scotia also have limited access if not to the technology (which some do, presumably based on family SES), then to high-speed service. Distance still does matter. It may be that the optimists are right and these divides will diminish as technology and Internet connections become more readily available. Nevertheless, the interim access issues in rural and remote areas are very real. As Hindman (2000, 557) notes: "The technological innovations of the information society do not eliminate the structural constraints associated with previous eras."

Further, as this analysis has shown, the issues are more complex than this. It is not just a matter of geographic location. Cultural location also matters. The patterns of access and use differ substantially between the Inuit and non-Inuit youth. Patterns of use and of skill development are heavily affected by home access, but there are other factors involved. In many instances rural–urban location still has a direct effect; in others cultural identity comes into play.

The pattern that appears is that context matters. This context includes not only physical, geographical location but one's social and cultural context. In the next chapter we explore the idea of distance from the cultural centre, examining ICT access, use, and skill development for four cultural groups within the sample. The current analysis shows that cultural distance and geographic distance interact in complex ways. This is most evident in the differences among the Inuit in different locales and in the differences among respondents depending on their geographic location.

This analysis also touched on the issue of cultural resistance to ICT. It is not clear from these data that the lower rates of access and use by the Inuit is a conscious matter of cultural resistance; however, it is important to recognize that it is not self-evident that higher use of ICT will necessarily serve the needs of the Inuit, if one of those needs is the preservation of traditional culture. Indeed, it may be that there are other pockets of resistance there and elsewhere, perhaps providing an explanation for urban Nova Scotia students having dial-up rather than high-speed Internet service.

As social scientists we need to critically examine the effects of ICT use on different cultural groups in different contexts. Under what circumstances is it an asset? When might it be a liability? When is it, in fact, used to bridge physical and cultural distance? When and by whom is it used to create bonds within and across these distances? The remaining chapters in this book explore these questions in more detail. Clearly, ongoing research is needed on this important topic. Next steps include an examination of some of the effects of higher use of ICT on other youth outcomes; for example, does it influence their educational and/or occupational plans and outcomes?

It is also, we feel, important to shift from a focus on the digital divides, real and as important as they are. It may be time instead to emphasize "digital diversity," recognizing that some of the diversity we see in the use of this technology does not always and only derive from disadvantage. It may be a valid choice. Nevertheless, it is clear from our analyses that distance is not "dead." There are still significant influences of location—both social and geographic—on access, use, and skill development with respect to ICT. Context matters.

NOTES

1 Statistics Canada defines rurality in terms of both concentration and dispersion of population: "persons living in sparsely populated lands lying outside of urban areas, i.e., persons living outside places of 1,000 people or more or outside places with population densities of 400 or more per square kilometer" (du Plessis et al. 2002, 1). Also of relevance can be the percentage who commute to a large urban centre (see discussion in du Plessis et al. 2002, 10). In any case, both size and distance from an urban centre are seen as the essence of a community being classified as rural.

2 If the respondent reported only one computer at home but listed time spent on their own and their family's computer, the computer on which they spent the longest time was counted and the other time ignored in the calculation of "total time spent on computers."

3 The one exception to this coding is that a school in one community that falls within the Halifax-Dartmouth metropolitan region is coded as rural given its distance from the central core area and the fact that, prior to the recent amalgamation, it was considered a rural area.

4 Note: all differences reported in the tables are statistically significant unless otherwise indicated.

5 The author would like to acknowledge the work that C. Croft has done in highlighting the importance of type of connectivity to this rural–urban analysis.

6 At the time of the survey, there was essentially no broadband or other high-speed Internet access in Nunavut. Since then broadband connections have been made available in all communities.

7   The effect of race and culture on ICT facility and use is examined in more detail in chapter 3.

8   Parental education is a not a useful measure of SES since the requirement for formal schooling in Nunavut is quite recent; 54% of fathers and 59% of mothers of these Nunavut students have less than high school. Virtually all (90%) or more of Nunavut respondents report having a telephone, television, VCR, washing machine, and CD player in their household. In other words there is not enough variation in these indicators to use them as a useful measure of SES. Having a digital camera differentiates households with access to higher levels of disposable income than those who do not so it was used as the admittedly limited measure of socio-economic status.

Works Cited

Alter, Theodore, Jeffrey Bridger, Sheila Sager, Kai Schafft, and Willima Shuffstall. 2007. "Getting Connected: Broadband Service a Key to a Vibrant Rural America." *Rural Realities* 2(1): 24–33.

Attewell, P. 2001. "The First and Second Digital Divides." *Sociology of Education* 74:252–59.

Cairncross, Frances. 1997. *The Death of Distance*. Boston: Harvard Business School Press.

Canadian Radio-television and Telecommunications Commission. 2006. "Monitoring Report: Status of Competition in Canadian Telecommunications Markets." Ottawa.

Compaine, M. Benjamin, ed. 2001. *The Digital Divide: Facing a Crisis or Creating a Myth?* Cambridge, MA: MIT Press.

du Plessis, Valerie, Roland Beshiri, Ray D. Bollman, and Heather Clemenson. 2002. "Definitions of Rural." Ottawa: Statistics Canada, Agriculture and Rural Working Paper No. 61, Catalogue no. 21-601-MIE.

Ferguson, C. 2004. "The Broadband Problem: Anatomy of a Market Failure and a Policy Dilemma." Washington: Brookings Institution Press.

Government of Canada. 2001. "Speech from the Throne." Ottawa.

———. 2001. "Response to the Speech from the Throne, Prime Minister Chrétien." Ottawa.

Hindman, Douglas Banks. 2000. "The Rural–Urban Digital Divide." *Journalism and Mass Communication Quarterly* 77(3): 549–60.

Industry Canada. 1996. "Connection, Community, Content: The Challenge of the Information Highway." Ottawa.

———. 2001. *The New National Dream: Networking the Nation for Broadband Access.* National Broadband Task Force. ftp://ftp.cordis.europa.eu/pub/ist/docs/ka4/mb_broadbandcanada.pdf.

———. 2006. "Canada's SchoolNet: What is SchoolNet?" http://web.archive.org/web/20070224224427/www.schoolnet.ca/home/e/whatis.asp.

Looker, E. Dianne and Victor Thiessen. 2003. 2003. "Beyond the Digital Divide in Canadian Schools: From Access to Competency in the Use of Information Technology." *Social Science Computer Review* 21:475–90.

Malecki, E. 2003. "Digital Development in Rural Areas: Potential and Pitfalls." *Journal of Rural Studies* 19:201–14.

McKeown, Larry, Anthony Noce, and Peter Czerny. 2007. "Factors Associated with Internet Use: Does Rurality Matter?" *Rural and Small Towns Analysis Bulletin.* Ottawa: Statistics Canada. Cat. #21-006-XIE.

McMullen, Bill and Andreas Rohrbach. 2003. *Distance Education in Remote Aboriginal Communities: Barriers, Learning Styles and Best Practices.* Prince George, BC: College of New Caledonia Press.

Mitchell, J. William. 2001. "The City of Bits Hypothesis." In *High Technology and Low-Income Communities: Prospects for the Positive Use of Advanced Information Technology*, ed. D. Schon, B. Sanyal, and W. Mitchell, 105–30. Cambridge, MA: MIT Press.

Natriello, G. 2001. "Bridging the Second Digital Divide: What Can Sociologists of Education Contribute?" *Sociology of Education* 74: 260–65.

Organization for Economic Co-operation and Development (OECD). 2001a. "Bridging the Digital Divide: Issues and Policies in OECD Countries." Paris: Organization for Economic Cooperation and Development. Pub. No. JT00110878.

———. 2001b. "Understanding the Digital Divide." Paris. http://www.oecd.org/dataoecd/38/57/1888451.pdf.

Ramírez, Ricardo. 2001. "A Model for Rural and Remote Information and Communication Technologies: A Canadian Exploration." *Telecommunications Policy* 25(5):315–30.

Reddick, Andrew, Christian Boucher, and Manon Groseilliers. 2006. "The Dual Digital Divide: The Information Highway in Canada." Public Interest Advocacy Centre and EKOS Research Associates.

Rideout, V. 2000. "Public Access to the Internet and the Canadian Digital Divide." *Canadian Journal of Information* and Library Science 25:1–21.

Sciadas, George. 2002. "Unveiling the Digital Divide." Ottawa: Statistics Canada.

Thiessen, Victor. 2007. "Performance and Perception: Exploring Gender Gaps in Human Capital Skills." *Canadian Journal of Sociology* 32 (2):145–76.

Thiessen, Victor and E. Dianne Looker. 2006. "Do New Communication Technologies Maintain or Erode Cultural Identity? The Experiences of Canadian Youth in Northern Communities, Indian Reserves, and among African Canadians." Paper presented at the International Sociological Association meetings. Durban, SA.

UNESCO. 2005. "Access to Information Essential to the Establishment of Knowledge Societies." http://portal.unesco.org/en/ev.php-URL_ID=16643&URL_DO= DO_TOPIC&URL_SECTION=201.html.

U.S. Department of Commerce. 1995. "Falling Through the Net: A Survey of the 'Have Nots' in Rural and Urban America." Washington, DC: National Telecommunications and Information Administration.
———. 1999. "Falling Through the Net: Defining the Digital Divide." Washington, DC: National Telecommunications and Information Administration.
———. 2004. "A Nation Online: Entering the Broadband Age." Washington, DC: National Telecommunications and Information Administration.

Chapter 3

Bridging and bonding social capital: Computer and Internet use among youth in relation to their cultural identities

Victor Thiessen

E. Dianne Looker

Computers and the Internet arguably represent the most important techno-logical innovations permeating Canadian classrooms since the introduction of textbooks. As indicated in the introductory chapter, all schools included in our student surveys were equipped with computers that students could (in principle) access. Although there are large differences in the extent of student access to ICT, all have been exposed to ICT to some extent. This chapter examines what roles computers and the Internet play in the lives of young people from different cultural and ethnic groups. Our overall interest is in examining how digital resources are used in young people's development of various types of capital, especially human and social capital. By focusing on the purposes for which ICT is used, we expressly recognize that ICT can serve many purposes and interests beyond its possible role in increasing human cap-ital skills. We are particularly interested in whether ICT, with its mixture of textual and graphic information, and its ability to connect people and infor-mation via the Internet, is more attractive to certain cultural and ethnic groups than others.

We examine four interrelated issues in this chapter, each with respect to similarities and differences between young people of different cultural iden-tities. First, how *effective* is the access to ICT between young people of differ-ent cultural identities? We consider effective access to ICT to have three components: (1) The physical capacity of the ICT configuration. Here the issue is especially whether computers and the Internet are available from home, since the review of the literature indicates that this is the primary site for student use of ICT. (2) The attitudes or dispositions students have toward ICT. Do students prefer classes in which ICT is used, or would they rather avoid such classes? Do they find their school work to be easier when computers are used? The mere physical availability of ICT is unlikely to translate into actual use without positive attitudes toward these learning mediums. (3) The extent of students' mastery of various ICT competencies and skills. There are many possible applications of ICT, each of which requires certain general or application-specific knowledge, such as how to download music or other types of files from the Internet. Effective access, we argue, presupposes a configuration that has sufficient technical capacity combined with favourable attitudes and beliefs about the potential benefits of this technology and the possession of sufficient ICT skills to be able to reap the potential benefits of this technology. The first section of our empirical analysis examines how these three components of effective ICT access are distributed across students with different cultural and ethnic identities.

The second issue is the relationship, from the student's vantage point, of computers to two other possible learning mediums: books and television. When students are given the choice, would they rather watch television, read a book, or use the computer? More importantly from an educational point of view, from which of these mediums do students believe they actually learn more? Are there cultural differences in these preferences and their perceived effectiveness?

Once these similarities and differences have been established, we turn our attention to the use of the Internet to develop bridging and bonding social capital. To what extent do young people use the Internet to connect with similar others (known as *bonding* social capital) and with dissimilar others (referred to as *bridging* capital)? In line with the overall theme of this chapter, similar others are defined as those with the same cultural identity. The questions relevant to our analysis of ICT focus on the ways it is used to create one or both types of social capital for youth. To what extent is the Internet used among Canadian young people to bond with others from their own cultural group? Presumably such communication with others of their own cultural group will serve to maintain young people's identity as a member of that group and in this way preserve their cultural heritage. Is the Internet used as a means to obtain information and make contact with other cultural groups and those with different life styles, and thereby create bridges to other groups?

The final issue we address is whether the Internet (and reliance on the English language) is implicated—or thought to be implicated—in the preservation or destruction of traditional cultures. In the Canadian context, although it was possible to use computers to communicate in Inuktitut (one of two main languages among the Inuit) at the time of our study, for example, this possibility was still in its infancy. Given also that two-thirds of the content on the Internet was in the English language at the time of our study (Mansell 2002), we felt it important to ascertain how high school students of different cultural identities felt about the relationship between their traditional culture and the Internet.

In this chapter we first review the relevant literature on each of the issues raised above. We then describe the various measures used in subsequent analyses to empirically explore these issues on the basis of our student surveys. We conclude with an empirical examination of the four issues and the implications of our findings on the role of ICT to enhance human and social capital among young Canadians of different cultural and ethnic identities.

REVIEW OF THE LITERATURE

Prior research on ICT access, use, and proficiency supports three important conclusions. First, although some digital divides in access, such as the gender gaps, have diminished in most developed countries (van Dijk 2006), racialized gaps in access, use, and skills persist and may even be increasing (Dimaggio et al. 2004; Jackson et al. 2006; Jones 2002; Lenhart, Madden, and Hitlin 2005; U.S. Department of Commerce 2000; Wasserman and Richmond-Abbott 2005). Second, although digital divides in material access may be declining, they are reappearing in newer forms, especially in frequency of use and mastery of a broad range of ICT skills (Gaved and Anderson 2006; Van Dijk and Hacker 2003). The prognosis is that the gaps in ICT skills will become more significant over time (Gaved and Anderson 2006; Van Dijk and Hacker 2003). Third, there is a growing recognition that a focus on digital divides is perhaps not as fruitful as one that emphasizes digital differentiation (Peter and Valkenburg 2006) or digital diversity. Digital diversity sensitizes scholars to the likelihood that individuals adapt technology use to meet their individual interests. Digital diversity in types of use reflects differences in life circumstances such as cultural, socio-economic, and cognitive resources. Further, a digital diversity approach predicts that even with equal material access to ICT, young people with different life interests will use this technology for distinct purposes. Thus, females, for whom social connections are typically important, are increasingly more likely than males to use the Internet for emails and chat rooms, for example (Colley and Comber 2003; Volman et al. 2005). One could imagine that visible minorities would be particularly attracted to the Internet for purposes of connecting with others from their own culture, as another example.

In line with our emphasis on *effective* access, Van Dijk and Hacker (2003) note that access to ICT has both a mental and a material component. The mental component includes a lack of interest in ICT, whether because of lack of confidence in one's ability to learn how to use ICT or lack of perceived need. In our work, we label this mental aspect "dispositions." Since access to ICT in both of these forms (material and mental) is a primary factor in subsequent use and proficiency, it is important to establish whether racialized groups differ in their acceptance of ICT generally as a useful tool and specifically as a learning medium. Differences between cultural groups in learning medium preferences can be expected from differences in access as well as from possible differences in learning styles. For example, in their work in isolated northern Canadian communities McMullen and Rohrbach (2003, 82), found that "Aboriginal students learn better by using images, symbols, and diagrams" and that oral traditions rather than printed materials were preferred. Likewise, Vandenberghe and Gierl (2001) postulated that Aboriginal communities emphasize different cognitive learning styles from those of non-Aboriginal learners. In particular, Aboriginal students are thought to rely more on simultaneous than on sequential information processing. Graphic images present information simultaneously, whereas textual material does so sequentially. Television presents information primarily in a graphic form, textbooks are heavily textual, and computers are especially suited to multimedia presentation of information. This chapter documents the extent to which the cultural groups in our study differ in their learning-medium preferences.

It is important to juxtapose young people's learning-medium preference structure against evidence of the effectiveness of watching television, reading books, and using computers for the acquisition of human capital. Empirical studies consistently document a negative relationship between the amount of time spent watching television and various measures of academic performance (Cooper et al. 1999; Fuligni and Stevenson 1995; Scott 2004). In con trast, what might be considered measures of a "reading culture," such as finding joy in reading and the number of books in the home, show positive associations with academic achievement even after controlling for parental socio-economic status and other factors associated with academic achievement (Frempong and Ma 2006; Jungbauer-Gans 2004; Wenglinsky 2003). Similarly, Thiessen (2008) documented that it was specifically the presence of books in the home, rather than other educational resources, such as computers or a study room of one's own, that was positively associated with literacy attainments. The effectiveness of ICT for improving learning outcomes remains debatable. Although some researchers have found positive relationships between ICT use and academic performance, the associations are modest at best (Bussière and Gluszynski 2004; Jackson et al. 2006; Sclater et al. 2006). A likely reason for the weak and inconsistent findings is that the relationship between ICT use and academic performance is not linear but rather curvilinear (in an inverted-U shape), suggesting an optimal level of computer use (Fuchs and Wößmann 2004; Thiessen and Looker 2007). To sum up, the evidence suggests that books remain the most effective learning medium, followed by moderate use of ICT, with time spent watching television being counterproductive. It should also be pointed out that the more time spent on any one of these activities results in less time spent on the others (Attewell, Suazo-Garcia, and Battle 2003; Gershuny 2003; Nie 2001).

In addition to documenting young people's learning-medium preferences, this chapter is interested in whether ICT in general and the Internet in particular serve as sources of social capital. As indicated previously, social capital refers to the development of the webs of connections people make with others that serve as vital resources for obtaining information or finding employment, for example.

Information and communication technology (ICT) is seen as having the potential to increase both bridging and bonding social capital (Pigg and Crank 2004). As a communications conduit, ICT can enhance the bonding within a subgroup, allowing for contact across distances and sharing of plans and activities. As Norris (2003, 6) notes, ICT and use of the Internet and online groups "is likely to strengthen social bonds among those with homogenous interests and backgrounds." Use of a common language is also likely to reinforce these bonds (Daniel et al. 2003). Bridging social capital, on the other hand, can be enhanced via the information component of ICT, allowing contact with resources and material not otherwise available. Norris's empirical analysis of survey data on Internet use concludes, however, that "participation in most online groups did little to bridge racial divides in America, other than contact with specific ethnic-cultural organizations" (2003, 9), raising questions about claims for the bridging functions of ICT.

In our analysis, bonding social capital is assumed to strengthen ties within a particular cultural group while bridging would create links between one of these groups and (a) other minority groups and, perhaps more importantly, (b) with those at the cultural centre. In terms of the racialized minorities we consider, some are particularly interested in seeking to strengthen and maintain strong bonding social capital. The Inuit and on-reserve First Nations peoples invest considerable energy in preserving their traditional culture and, where possible, their language; for example, there are Internet resources dedicated to providing culturally relevant information to First Nations and Inuit young people. The Aboriginal Youth Network (http://www.ayn.ca/index.html), with its motto "Connecting the hearts and minds of Aboriginal youth worldwide" is operated by Aboriginal youth themselves. It emphasizes the importance of sharing information about their culture and traditions. Industry Canada, through its First Nations SchoolNet program (http://www.firstnationsnt.ca/) provides Internet access to First Nations schools. The Atlantic Canada First Nation Help Desk (http://www.firstnationhelp.com/) has numerous lessons for learning Aboriginal language.

Ties to the dominant culture by minority groups are perhaps developed with more ambivalence. Such ties may be needed for economic development, but there is recognition of the danger to traditional cultures posed by these ties. In other words, we would expect members of these groups but not, for example, Black youth, to emphasize the development of bonding rather than bridging social capital, given their concern with reducing discrimination (i.e., being accepted as similar to whites).

The Internet was developed in the first instance as an English-language medium. Language is a contentious issue for racialized groups whose first language is not English. Although some progress has arguably been made in non-English Internet sites and resources (compare the figures cited by Cuneo 2002 and Mansell 2002), the question remains about the extent to which young people communicate on the Internet with each other and find information in their first language. Our survey of high school students in Canada will help illuminate these issues by examining how often they engage in these activities in their own language as compared to in the English language. These comparisons will provide a first indication of whether the Internet is a medium conducive to the retention of young people's own language or whether it remains in practice primarily an English-language medium.

There is some debate about whether the Internet acts as a homogenizing influence, breaking down cultural integrities, or whether it provides a means for strengthening traditional cultures. Limited research indicates that within ethnic groups, those who are most committed to preserving their traditional way of life are also the least likely to use ICT or to equip their homes with such technologies (Thiessen and Looker 2008). Do students from different racialized minorities feel the Internet is a threat to their culture, or do they see it as a resource that will help preserve their cultural heritage?

DESCRIPTION OF THE MEASURES

The data in this chapter reflect the responses of over 2,500 students in Grades 9 to 12 who participated in the student surveys described in the introductory chapter of this book. What we present is the picture gleaned from these student responses, with the caution that these pictures are not necessarily "facts." They remain student perceptions, with all the ambiguities and contradictions that emerge whenever one asks humans about their attitudes and behaviours. We must keep in mind the Thomas dictum, however: That which is perceived as real is real in its consequences.[1] Here we provide the descriptions of the variables used in this analysis.

Cultural identity

The usefulness and/or appropriateness of the concepts of race, ethnicity, and cultural identity remain contested; nevertheless, they are crucial for understanding the role of ICT among young people. We have opted to approach this issue from a self-identification perspective. Our sampling design contributed to making this approach relatively straightforward and non-contentious for most of the students. In Nunavut, students strongly identified themselves as Inuit, except for the small number of Europeans whose parents came to work there. In Nova Scotia, most of the First Nations youth in our study were living on reserves, and identity as a member of First Nations people was not problematic for them. We also employed an African Nova Scotian facilitator to meet with African Nova Scotian students in several high schools as a way of increasing the participation rate of this visible minority. The facilitator indicated that these students were comfortable describing themselves as African Nova Scotian.

In the survey cultural identity was tapped through the question "Which of the following terms would you use to best describe yourself?" Response options included: African Canadian, Other African descent, Mi'kmaq, Inuit, Other First Nations, Asian Canadian, Other Asian Descent, White, and Other. African Canadian and Other African descent were combined into one category (classified as "Black"), as were Mi'kmaq and Other First Nations, as well as Asian Canadian and Other Asian Descent. Although students were instructed to select only one, some youth provided multiple responses, while for a few others, no response was given. To maximize both the total number of usable responses and to obtain sufficient numbers of non-White group members, the following decisions were made: (1) If a student indicated two or more racialized identities, they were assigned to the group considered more distant from the cultural centre (that is, from Whites; see Thiessen and Looker 2008). (2) If no response was given to the question and the school was located in Nunavut, the student was classified as Inuit. (3) If no response was given and the school was located on a reserve, the student was classified as First Nations. (4) Responses of "Other" and all other non-response to the self-identification question were classified as White. By these criteria, the sample contained 526 Inuit, 154 First Nations (almost exclusively on-reserve), 149 African Canadian, 56 Asian,[2] and 1,642 White students. Although cultural identities can be fluid and complex, the simplified categories constructed for the analyses in this chapter appear to capture some important differences on the issues being examined in this chapter.

ICT access, attitudes, and skills

Information on home access to ICT was elicited through two questions: the number of computers in the home and the nature of any Internet connection (none, dial-up, high-speed). Responses were combined to create a five-point index of home ICT configuration, ranging from no computers at home at the low end to two or more computers with high-speed Internet connection at the high end.

Responses to six statements tap students' dispositions to computers:

- I prefer courses where I get to use computers.
- I would avoid a course if I had to use a computer in it.
- I will be able to get a better job if I learn how to use a computer.

- I feel comfortable working with a computer.
- I get annoyed when I use a computer.
- School work is easier with a computer.

These items had a five-point Likert response format ranging from strongly disagree to strongly agree. After reversing the coding for those items that had opposite polarities, a summary measure consisting of the mean of the six items was constructed. Cronbach's alpha (a measure of reliability based on internal consistency) for this scale is 0.68.

We have two measures of ICT competence. One involves asking the students to rate themselves on a scale from 1 to 7 (with 7 being "expert"). This item might be considered a measure of confidence in their computer skills, since previous research indicates that females, for example, rate themselves lower on similar items than do males, even after controlling for extent of ICT use (Bunz, Curry, and Voon 2006; Chan et al. 2000; Volman and van Eck 2001). For the second measure, students were asked to assess their competence on nineteen specific ICT tasks. Typical items were:

- Cut, copy, and paste information from one place to another
- Choose the font size and type of text, and **bold**, *italic*, and <u>underline</u>
- Use spell-check
- Send an attachment with an e-mail
- Make charts or graphs in a spreadsheet
- Make a web page that has words and pictures

Four response options, ranging from "I don't know how to do this" (scored as 1) to "I can teach others how to do this" (scored as 4) were provided. The mean of the responses to the nineteen items constitutes our summary measure of ICT skills. Cronbach's alpha for this scale is 0.95.

Learning mediums

The three most important learning mediums today are, arguably, computers, books, and TV. In the survey, paired comparisons between these three mediums (watch TV or use a computer; use a computer or read a book; read a book or watch TV) were obtained with respect to two issues: which medium would they rather use, and from which medium do they believe they learn more. Although we forced the students to choose between the three mediums in pairs, our observations during the data collection phase revealed that substantial numbers of youth experienced difficulty making such choices. Consequently, a total of 340 students failed to answer this series of questions. There is also some reason to believe that young people who are attracted to ICT are also more likely to spend time reading books (Mesch 2001), and their difficulty to choose between these mediums may have been a manifestation of this. To provide a summary measure of learning preferences, responses to the three paired comparisons were combined into three outcomes: (1) working with computers was selected over either reading books or watching TV, (2) watching TV was selected over either working with computers or reading books, and (3) reading books was selected over either working with computers or watching TV. An additional 119 preference responses, and 149 learning responses, were intransitive (for example, preferred computers over television, television over reading, but preferred reading over computers), and these are treated as missing values in order to focus on those students who provided us with clear choices.

FINDINGS
ICT access, use, and skills
Due to the efforts of provincial, territorial, and federal governments, there is essentially universal access and use of ICT in schools. That is, there are no appreciable racialized differences in the extent to which computers are available in schools, although our field work made us recognize that maintaining ICT in good working order was substantially more problematic in Nunavut than in Nova Scotia. What must be remembered in this context, however, is that students use home-based ICT much more than school-based ICT (Levin and Arafeh 2002). Hence, schools are limited in the extent to which they can minimize racialized digital divides, although Attewell (2001) reviews several studies that show racialized minorities to use school-based ICT more frequently than their White counterparts.

There are huge racialized inequalities in both home computers and Internet access, however (Figure 3.1). Inuit youth were least likely to have a computer in their home (only 57% had one). Most Black and Mi'kmaq respondents were likely to live in a home equipped with at least one computer (85% and 88% respectively), and the same was true for virtually all Asian and White youth (98% and 97%, respectively). Similar differences were found with Internet connections. Only 43% of the Inuit, compared to 82% of Black, 88% of Mi'kmaq, 96% of Asian, and 95% of White respondents

FIGURE 3.1

Home ICT configuration by cultural identity

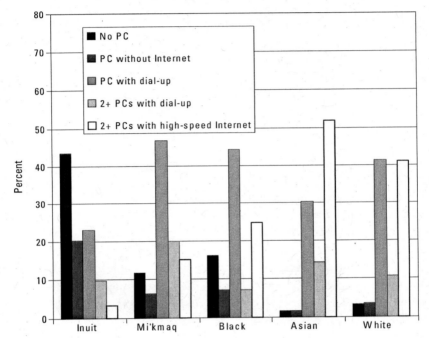

had either a dial-up or a high-speed connection to the Internet in their home. Over a quarter (27%) of the variance in home ICT configuration was accounted for by racialized inequalities.

Given the racialized inequalities in home ICT configuration, it is to be expected that self-reported competence and the skill index would mirror the differences in home ICT. As we can see in Table 3.1, both measures (columns 1 and 2) show the expected differences by racial/cultural group: 15% of the variance in self-assessed skills and over one-third (35%) of the variance in our skill index is associated with membership in the different population groups.

These inequalities form a consistent pattern of the following kind: Access to ICT at home, as well as skill levels of various ICT tasks and self-assessed competence, are lowest among Inuit students, followed in order by Mi'kmaq, Black, and Asian students; Asian respondents are essentially identical to White in both home ICT access and level of ICT skills.

TABLE 3.1

Mean ICT competence, skill, and disposition by cultural identity

Cultural identity	Self-reported competence	Skill index	Disposition	N*
Inuit	4.07	2.16	3.73	515
Mi'kmaq	4.95	2.83	3.74	154
Black	5.14	3.05	3.88	148
Asian	5.22	3.30	3.88	56
White	5.29	3.27	3.95	1619

* Due to missing values, the number of cases varies slightly between the three variables.

Inuit < Mi'kmaq < Black < Asian ≈ White

Much of the difference in ICT skills can be traced back to inequalities in home access; however, substantial racialized differences remain even after controlling for home ICT resources and parental socio-economic status (data not shown).

Compared to racialized differences in ICT skill levels, disparities in attitudes toward ICT as measured by our disposition index are modest, with only 2% of the variance in dispositions associated with population group membership. That is, young people, regardless of their cultural identities, tend to have relatively positive attitudes toward ICT. What little difference there is in attitudes, takes the following rank order:

Inuit ≈ Mi'kmaq < Black = Asian < White
3.73 ≈ 3.74 < 3.88 = 3.88 < 3.95

It is also important to note that racialized differences in ICT skill levels are substantially greater than differences in the amount of time using ICT between the different cultural groups (data not shown). This finding implies that ICT is used more effectively in some groups than in others.

Having examined the patterns relating to access, skills, and dispositions, we now look at how the young people in our sample feel about three possible learning mediums: books, television, and computers.

Learning medium preferences

It is well known that young people spend much time watching television (Arnett 2002). We were therefore interested to determine to what extent

FIGURE 3.2

Learning medium preferences by cultural identity

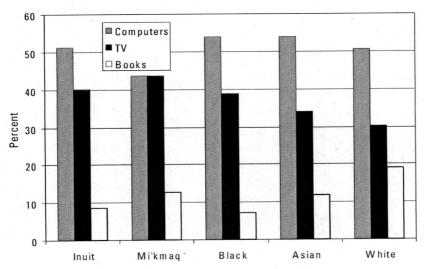

using computers might compete with watching TV. Surprisingly, in all population groups, working on a computer is the most preferred activity (among Mi'kmaq, working on a computer is tied with watching TV; see Figure 3.2). For all population groups, watching television is in second place and reading books a distant third. Although the differences between the population groups are modest (the maximum difference between population groups for any activity preference is 13%), they are statistically significant. It is interesting to note that a higher proportion of White students than any other group preferred reading books (although it is still the case that reading books is preferred by less than a fifth of them), and watching television is less preferred by them than by any other group. Combining working with computers and watching television as graphic methods, Black and Inuit youth are most attracted to graphic methods (93% and 91%, respectively).

Immediately after answering the question about what they would rather do, students were asked from which medium they think they would learn more, again with the same paired comparisons: watching TV or using a computer; using a computer or reading a book; reading a book or watching TV. Figure 3.3 shows the results.

Remarkably, about half the students believe that they learn more using computers than they do from either reading books or watching TV. However, in contrast to their preferences, substantially more young people believe that they learn more from reading books than they do from watching TV—a belief that is congruent with the evidence provided earlier. In fact, in all cultural groups, the rank order of learning mediums is that: ICT > Books > TV, although among Mi'kmaq, Black, and Inuit students, learning from books is close to being tied with learning from television. Note also that among the two groups that enjoy the best home ICT configuration (Asians and Whites) there is also the greatest appreciation that one learns more from books than from computers. In both of these groups there is also the least tendency to believe that one learns more from TV than from either books or computers. These cultural differences in perceptions about learning mediums are potentially of great importance, since other research consistently shows that Asian and White students perform better scholastically than Black, First Nations, and Inuit students. This is particularly important in light of the fact that Black students, for example, spend more time watching television than White students (Muller and Kerbow 1993). At the same time, these findings support the possibility that graphic methods are particularly effective learning mediums for First Nations and Inuit youth.

FIGURE 3.3

Perceived effectiveness of learning mediums by cultural identity

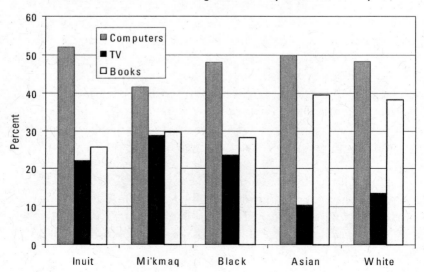

Bonding and bridging social capital

What do the student responses tell us about how the Internet is used for both bonding and bridging social capital? Students were asked how often in the past month they had used three types of materials to obtain information about their own cultural group and each of the other minority cultural groups that we have been discussing. The three types of materials were: (1) books, pamphlets, other print materials from school, (2) educational software from their school, and (3) the Internet outside of school. To simplify the presentation we present whether they have used these sources at least once in the past month.

Turning first to obtaining information about their own cultural group, we see that in all racialized groups except Asian Canadians, print material provided in the school is more likely to have been used for information about their own cultural group than either educational software or the Internet. This is surprising given the findings in the previous section concerning young people's medium preferences. Although young people may prefer computers over other media, and although they may feel they learn more through ICT, they nevertheless still rely more on school-provided printed materials for information about their own cultural group. Clearly, among high school students the Internet has not supplanted the printed word as the medium through

FIGURE 3.4

Accessed information on *own* cultural group in the last month

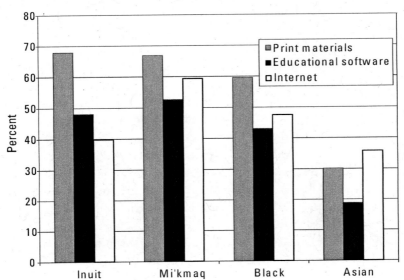

which information about one's own cultural group is obtained. Nevertheless, the Internet appears to be a close runner-up, except among the Inuit. It appears then, that there is potential for the Internet to supplement the bonding activities within minority groups, at least in terms of obtaining information about one's culture.

Books, pamphlets, and other print material provided through their schools are especially likely to be used in schools serving Inuit and First Nations students. This is not surprising since in our sample of schools, those serving Inuit and Mi'kmaq students were the most homogeneous with respect to cultural identities of the students. Black and Asian Canadian students were enrolled in schools in which they were a distinct minority. Asian Canadians are not well represented in any of the sample schools, and it is likely that this is the reason that they are the least likely to have obtained information about their own group from school-provided resources. It is quite likely that we would have had different findings had we conducted our study in Vancouver, for example, where the proportion of Asian students is much higher.

Bridging with other cultural groups

Turning to bridging social capital, three points stand out (see Figure 3.5). First, for all three types of learning material, accessing information about other cultural groups is less likely to occur than accessing information about one's own cultural group (compare the percentages from Figure 3.5 to those in Figure 3.4). The notable exception is for Asian students, who are more likely to obtain bridging information than bonding information from each of the three sources. In short, bridging social capital is less prevalent than bonding social capital (except among Asian students).

Second, books, pamphlets, and other print materials provided by schools remains the primary source of information about other cultural groups for all cultural groups (the first bar in each triplet is the tallest). Here, too, the Internet has not supplanted print materials as a source of bridging information. Why hasn't it? Our field work suggests that many of the students have the prerequisite skills to accomplish such tasks and often perform similar tasks on topics they happen to be particularly interested in but for which they cannot obtain the information through the school. So, for example, some students reported enthusiastically to us how they used the Internet to obtain and download the guitar chords for popular songs. In situations where the school

FIGURE 3.5

Accessed information about *other* cultural groups in the last month

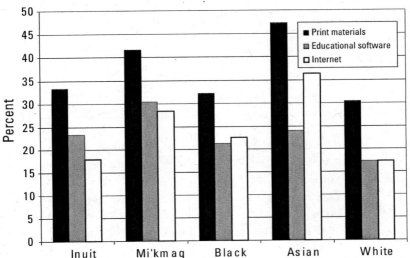

already provides the information in print, there is little reason for students to search for it on the Internet.

Third, White students are the least likely to have used any of the three sources of information about other cultural groups; that is, each of the three bars for the White students is shorter than the corresponding bars for each of the other racialized groups. If we consider Whites to be the cultural "centre" (see Thiessen and Looker 2006), it appears that the Internet is used more to provide information to those outside the centre than to provide information to those at the centre about other groups.

The Internet and cultural preservation

We come now to the question of whether young people see the Internet as helping to preserve their traditional culture or whether they see it as a threat to their culture. The first answer is that it is seen as neither, since the most popular response among students of each of the cultural groups is that the Internet is neutral with respect to traditional culture. Table 3.2 shows that between two-fifths and three-fifths of students of the various cultural groups hold this point of view. Among the remainder, Inuit, Mi'kmaq, and White students are more likely to believe that the Internet will be detrimental to

TABLE 3.2

Traditional culture and the Internet

Percent who believe the Internet	Inuit	Mi'kmaq	Black	Asian	White
Will help preserve traditional culture	18	23	25	27	15
Is neutral with respect to traditional culture	48	40	60	52	59
Will make us lose our traditional culture	35	37	15	21	25
Total	100	100	100	100	100

their culture than that it will help preserve it. In contrast, Asian and Black students are more likely to feel that the Internet will help preserve rather than make them lose their traditional culture.

All in all, it is probably best to conclude that young people do not hold strong views about either the positive or negative future effects of the Internet on their culture. It is interesting, however, that the two groups (the Inuit and the Mi'kmaq) who are, as we said earlier, making concerted efforts to maintain their separate, traditional culture, are more likely than the others to see the Internet as potentially detrimental.

First language and Internet activities

The final issue we will address is the role of language in the use of the Internet for a variety of activities. Students were asked what the first language was they learned to speak. Their responses were recoded into English–not English for this part of the analysis. They were subsequently asked (a) how often they talked with someone in their first language on the Internet, (b) how often they talked with someone from their own cultural group on the Internet, (c) how often they found information for their school on the Internet in their first language, and (d) how often they found other information on the Internet in their first language. In Table 3.3, we report the percentages who said they did these things at least a few times each week.

Looking at the first two rows of the table, we see that in all cultural groups, those whose first language is English are more likely to have talked with someone in their first language than are those whose first language is not English. The differences by first language are substantial for all cultural groups except among the Mi'kmaq, where the difference is only three percentage points. Clearly language is an important factor for this Internet activ-

TABLE 3.3

Communication via the Internet by first language

Activity	Language	Inuit	Mi'kmaq	Black	Asian	White
Talk with someone in their first language (%)						
	English	56	74	89	81	86
	Other	31	71	53	55	30
Talk with someone from their own cultural group (%)						
	English	37	63	81	44	73
	Other	24	70	47	48	31
Find information for their school in their first language (%)						
	English	38	51	70	67	64
	Other	12	34	29	28	16
Find other information in their first language (%)						
	English	44	50	74	70	77
	Other	13	34	47	45	23

Note: Numbers indicate the percent who said they did a given activity at least a few times a week.

ity. Reflecting back on whether the Internet helps preserve traditional culture, these findings suggest that it does not, since those who are most steeped in traditional culture (as measured by their first language) are least likely to use the Internet to communicate with others in their language.

Comparing rows three and four we see that language makes a substantial difference on whether or not one frequently talks with someone from one's own cultural group in some cultural groups, but not in others. Thus among Inuit, Black, and White students, those whose first language is English are substantially more likely to talk frequently with someone from their own cultural group. In contrast, among Mi'kmaq and Asian students there is a slight tendency for those whose first language is not English to talk frequently with others from their own cultural group. Here we see a hint of the Mi'kmaq students using the Internet to maintain within-group connections.

The remaining rows of Table 3.3 reinforce the conclusion that the Internet is primarily an English-language medium. For all cultural groups, and regardless of whether the Internet is used to search for school-related information or other information, students whose first language is English are substantially more likely to use the Internet for these purposes than are students whose first language is not English. The unavoidable conclusion is that a lot of effort will be required to make information more easily accessible to Canadian students whose first language is not English. And if learning is more effective in an environment that is sensitive to the language of the learners, then it follows that it will take some time before the Internet can serve as a medium to reduce current learning inequalities.

SUMMARY AND CONCLUSION

This chapter has covered a wide range of issues with respect to how ICT is used for information and for communicating by youth from the different racialized groups in our study. We look at access, dispositions, and use (effective access), attitudes to different learning mediums, use of ICT for bridging and bonding with members of different groups, and the effects of ICT on cultural preservation, especially in terms of language. We cover this range of topics to document that the issues facing different cultural and racial groups are complex, not simply a matter of specific types of digital divides based on race. To reduce it to this conclusion would be simplistic and would ignore the multifaceted components of the experiences of these different groups.

As we outlined in the introductory chapter to this book, there was a reason for our choosing the groups we did and for sampling particular types of schools. First Nations groups (including the Mi'kmaq represented in the band school we chose), although numerically a minority, have official status and rights as well as separate schools on their reserves. Although there is no doubt they are disadvantaged in a host of ways, they do have this official status and recognition and organizations designed to maintain and promote their traditional culture and well-being. African Canadians and others of African descent are also a minority and no less disadvantaged in many ways, but they have no such official status. Many of their organizations are designed to reduce the discrimination they face in their day-to-day lives. The Inuit in Nunavut, although a minority in Canada as a whole are very much the majority in their territory. Further, they have a government whose mandate clearly includes preservation of their culture. We did not explicitly sample youth of Asian descent, but there are sufficient numbers of them in the schools we included to identify them and provide a contrast with both White students as the dominant group and these other racialized minorities. In this study, as in few others, we have information from not just one racialized group but several. The locations and experiences of youth in these different groups are varied, reflecting differences not only in their cultural backgrounds but also in their structural locations in Canadian society. Ignoring these differences by lumping these young people together as "minority youth" would mask the diverse and complex interactions they have with ICT. So, what effect do these different structural locations have on youth access to and use of ICT for communicating and for gathering information, for school and for other activities?

First of all, we see some important differences in what we call the effective access of youth in these groups to ICT. There *are* digital divides in physical access to the technology. This comes as no surprise to anyone familiar with the literature on race and ICT. But what we are focusing on here is not simply the difference between the White youth and all others but the important variations among all the groups. Despite the official mandates of the organizations responsible for Mi'kmaq and Inuit youth, they do not have access to ICT infrastructure that comes anywhere near matching that available to White youth. Some of this access limitation can be attributed to the fact that these groups are concentrated in rural schools in our sample. However, as documented in chapter 2, this is not the whole story, at least for Inuit youth. Further it does not explain the access differences between Black youth on the one hand and Asian and White youth on the other. It does raise some important questions on how resources for ICT are distributed. Both Black and Asian students (and two thirds of White students) in our sample are concentrated in urban areas, so the technology could be made available. What is more, controlling on socio-economic status does not erase these racialized differences. Since the issue here is home access, the question becomes why Asian (and White) families are more willing to invest in this technology than those of Black students. The link may be to education, since it is well documented that Asian Canadians have high educational aspirations (and attainments), while Canadian Black students still lag behind White and Asian students in their attainments. If parents see ICT as facilitating their child's educational performance, then those who anticipate higher returns may be more willing to make this investment. Unfortunately our survey has no information on parental educational preferences for their child. Although further research is needed to explore this issue, it does raise the question of how schools and community groups can assist Black youth by providing more access to ICT, especially given that the dispositions of Black youth to ICT is similar to those for White and Asian youth. That is, there is little evidence of resistance to ICT on the part of Black youth.

Not surprisingly, the group patterns for skill development and for self-reported levels of competence with ICT parallel the access divides. In other words, if the hype about the importance of skills using ICTs for successful participation in the knowledge economy is at all accurate, these results suggest that Black, First Nations and Inuit youth are not being well served. They will be facing the challenge of entering and participating in this more knowledge-based economy with fewer skills and less confidence than their White counterparts. This alone is an equity issue that needs addressing.

However, our analysis goes far beyond providing further documentation of this now well-known digital divide. One aspect we cover, which focuses on the information-gathering capacities of ICT, deals with the learning mediums that the youth use and prefer. Without repeating the details presented above, we note that computers are preferred by more youth than either television or books. Nevertheless, the large numbers of White youth who prefer books suggests they may have a further educational edge since, as the literature we reviewed above argues, an emphasis on books in the home appears to facilitate higher levels of educational attainment. Interestingly, in all groups, more youth also seem to think they learn more using ICT than either television or books. If one considers both ICT and television as visual or graphic media, then these methods might be more effective for the Inuit and Mi'kmaq youth. Given the fact that one rationale for the high levels of investment in ICT in the schools was to help transform pedagogical practices to be more effective for the diverse body of students in today's classrooms (a claim that will be explored in more detail in later chapters) our results suggest that this technology can be used more effectively, particularly for certain students. These results are all the more important when one takes into account the relatively low levels of academic achievement for First Nations and Inuit groups. Perhaps more effective use of ICT and other graphic methods in the curriculum can help counter this pattern and enhance the human capital of Aboriginal youth in Canada.

As we discussed in earlier chapters, ICT can also be used to create and strengthen social capital; so we examined the patterns of ICT use for gathering information about and for communicating with those in one's own cultural group and with others. Despite the beliefs of these youth that they learn more using ICT than print media, most of the information they access about their own cultural group, and about those in other groups, is from print media, specifically print media provided by the school. Rarely is educational software the source of this information; however, more of the Inuit youth access educational software for this information than use the Internet outside of school. This pattern undoubtedly reflects a number of different factors: their limited access to the Internet, especially high-speed Internet, outside school, lack of material on the Internet about the Inuit, and language barriers. Nevertheless, the lack of use of educational software raises questions about the development of this software. The students' use of print material provided by the school indicates that schools *do* have access to relevant material about different cultural groups and that they see it as a sufficient priority to make it available to students. Why then is there not more ICT-based curricular material available, making use of both the multimedia format to keep student interest and the graphic content that may be more amenable to many young people? Another concern is the availability of culturally relevant material. An example from our field work illustrates the importance of culturally relevant material in the curriculum as delivered. In one First Nations high school, our Mi'kmaq research facilitator attended a class in which the instructor was teaching the students how to download a picture of Shakespeare as part of the class lesson. After the class, the facilitator asked the teacher whether it might not have been more appropriate or effective to download a picture or information about someone like Rita Joe, a local Mi'kmaq poet. The (White) teacher replied with some chagrin that it had simply never crossed his mind. It may well be that this was not an isolated example, but part of the pattern where English-language, European-focused material is both more prevalent and more likely to be part of the formal school curriculum even in schools that serve primarily students with a non-White cultural identity. Under such circumstances, it is not surprising that these students come to see the Internet as potentially detrimental to their traditional culture. Further, taking into account the low levels reported by White students using any of the different materials to access information about other groups, we raise the question of how the educational use of ICT and of other media is going to enhance equity if those who are privileged by the existing inequities are not informed about others.

This point leads us to a related issue. Ostensibly one way to enhance equity between disparate groups is to minimize the disparities; however, when one is focusing, as we are here, on groups with different cultural traditions, the issue becomes more complex. Canadians have a checkered history when it comes to attempts to assimilate both First Nations and other minority groups. With formal apologies from governments and reparations to survivors, perhaps we now understand that many Canadians with cultures other than those derived from European origins, including the growing number of Aboriginal peoples, want *not* to assimilate but to preserve and enhance their traditional cultures and languages. Can and does ICT facilitate this process or is it one more form of assault on these traditions?

Our results suggest that most youth, including those from the two Aboriginal groups we sampled, see ICT and the Internet as irrelevant to this issue of cultural preservation. The one counterpoint to this result is the fact that more of these Aboriginal students than those in other groups see the Internet as a potential threat to their culture. Presumably it need not inherently be a threat, if their culture and traditions are more represented and if their language becomes more accessible on the Internet. Given the diversity of languages and cultures included in the term "Aboriginal" in Canada, it is questionable how likely this development is in the near future.

Further, we would argue that it is not self-evident that more exposure to the Internet will benefit these youth. The dilemma they face, one that is not an issue to the dominant White group, is that they may have to choose between actively joining the so-called "information society" or maintaining their culture and traditions by insulating themselves from this technology. The fact that members of the different groups we studied were more likely to use the Internet to communicate with others in their own cultural group if their first language was English, highlights this fact. Nevertheless, the counterpoint to this conclusion is that Mi'kmaq youth whose first language was other than English use the Internet for this function more than their English-raised counterparts. This gives a hint that the Internet might be appropriated by these cultural groups to serve their own purposes. At this stage we can only offer these hints as an indication that ICT can be and sometimes is used to enhance equity rather than entrench inequities among Canadian youth.

NOTES

1 Formulated in 1928 by the sociologist William Isaac Thomas.
2 It is well known that there are large cultural differences among Asians with respect to educational outcomes generally, with East Asians exhibiting higher academic performance than other Asians. The small number of Asian youth in our sample prohibits making finer distinctions. In addition, the differences among Asians on these topics are substantially fewer than those between this group and the other visible minorities.

WORKS CITED

Arnett, Jeffrey Jensen. 2002. "Adolescents in Western Countries in the 21st century: Vast Opportunities—for All?" in *The World's Youth: Adolescence in Eight Regions of the Globe*, ed. B.B. Brown, R.W. Larson, and T.S. Saraswathi, 307–43. Cambridge: Cambridge University Press.

Attewell, P. 2001. "The First and Second Digital Divides." *Sociology of Education* 74:252–59.

Attewell, Paul, Belkis Suazo-Garcia, and Juan Battle. 2003. "Computers and Young Children: Social Benefit or Social Problem." *Social Forces* 82:277–96.

Bunz, Ulla, Carey Curry, and William Voon. 2006. "Perceived versus Actual Computer–Email–Web Fluency." *Computers in Human Behavior* 23:2321–44.

Bussière, Patrick and Tomasz Gluszynski. 2004. "The Impact of Computer Use on Reading Achievement of 15-year-olds." Ottawa: Human Resources and Skills Development Canada.

Chan, Vania, Katie Stafford, Maria Klawe, and Grace Chen. 2000. "Gender Difference in Vancouver Secondary Students' Interests Related to Information Technology Careers." In *Women, Work and Computerization: Charting a Course to the Future*, ed. E. Balka and R. Smith, 58–69. Boston: Kluwer Academic Publishers.

Colley, Ann and Chris Comber. 2003. "Age and Gender Differences in Computer Use and Attitudes among Secondary School Students: What Has Changed?" *Educational Research* 45:155–65.

Cooper, Harris, Jeffrey C. Valentine, Barbara Nye, and James J. Lindsay. 1999. "Relationships between Five After-school Activities and Academic Achievement." *Journal of Educational Psychology* 91:369–78.

Cuneo, Carl. 2002. "Globalized and Localized Digital Divides along the Information Highway: A Fragile Synthesis across Bridges, Ramps, Cloverleaves, and Ladders." The 33rd Annual Sorokin Lecture, University of Saskatchewan. 31 January. http://socserv2.mcmaster.ca/sociology/Digital-Divide-Sorokin-4.pdf.

Daniel, Ben, Richard A. Schweir, and Gordon McCalla. 2003. "Social Capital in Virtual Learning Communities and Distributed Communities of Practice." *Canadian Journal of Learning and Technology* 29:113–39.

Dimaggio, Paul, Eszter Hargittai, Coral Celeste, and Steven Shafer. 2004. "From Unequal Access to Differentiated Use: A Literature Review and Agenda for Research on Digital Inequality." New York: Russell Sage Foundation.

Frempong, George and Xin Ma. 2006. "Improving Reading Skills: Policy Sensitive Non-School and Family Factors." Ottawa: HRSDC.

Fuchs, Thomas and Ludger Wößmann. 2004. "Computers and Student Learning: Bivariate and Multivariate Evidence on the Availability and Use of Computers at Home and at School." CESifo Working Paper Series No. 1321. http://ssrn.com/abstract=619101.

Fuligni, Andrew J. and Harold W. Stevenson. 1995. "Time Use and Mathematics Achievement among American, Chinese, and Japanese High School Students." *Child Development* 66:830–42.

Gaved, Mark and Ben Anderson. 2006. "The Impact of Local ICT Initiatives on Social Capital and Quality of Life." Colchester: University of Essex, Chimera Working Paper 2006-6.

Gershuny, Jonathan. 2003. "Web Use and Net Nerds: A Neofunctionalist Analysis of the Impact of Information Technology in the Home." *Social Forces* 82:141–68.

Jackson, Linda A., Alexander von Eye, Frank A. Biocca, Gretchen Barbatsis, Yong Zhao, and Hiram E. Fitzgerald. 2006. "Does Home Internet Use Influence the Academic Performance of Low-income Children?" *Developmental Psychology* 42:429–35.

Jones, Steve. 2002. "The Internet Goes to College: How Students Are Living in the Future with Today's Technology." Washington, DC: Pew Internet & American Life Project, 4 September.

Jungbauer-Gans, Monika. 2004. "The Influence of Social and Cultural Capital on Reading Achievement: An International Comparison of the PISA 2000-Data." Paper presented at the American Sociological Association annual meetings, San Francisco.

Lenhart, Amanda, Mary Madden, and Paul Hitlin. 2005. "Teens and Technology." Washington, DC: PEW Internet and American Life Project.

Levin, Douglas and Sousan Arafeh. 2002. "The Digital Disconnect: The Widening Gap between Internet-savvy Students and Their Schools." Washington, DC: Pew Internet and American Life Project.

Mansell, Robin. 2002. "From Digital Divides to Digital Entitlements in Knowledge Societies." *Current Sociology* 50:407–26.

McMullen, Bill and Andreas Rohrbach. 2003. *Distance Education in Remote Aboriginal Communities: Barriers, Learning Styles and Best Practices*. Prince George, BC: College of New Caledonia Press.

Mesch, Gustavo S. 2001. "Social Relationships and Internet Use among Adolescents in Israel." *Social Science Quarterly* 82:329–39.

Muller, Chandra and David Kerbow. 1993. "Parent Involvement in the Home, School, and Community." In *Parents, Their Children, and Schools*. ed. B. Schneider and J. S. Coleman, 13–42. Boulder, CO: Westview.

Nie, Norman H. 2001. "Sociability, Interpersonal Relations, and the Internet." *American Behavioral Scientist* 45:420–35.

Norris, Pippa. 2003. "Social Capital and ICTs: Widening or Reinforcing Social Networks." Paper presented at the International Forum on Social Capital for Economic Revival, March 24–25, Tokyo, Japan.

Peter, Jochen and Patti M. Valkenburg. 2006. "Adolescents' Internet Use: Testing the 'Disappearing Digital Divide' versus the 'Emerging Digital Differentiation' Approach." *Poetics* 34:296–305.

Pigg, Kenneth E. and Laura Duffy Crank. 2004. "Building Community Social Capital: The Potential and Promise of Information and Communication Technologies." *Journal of Community Informatics* 1:58–73.

Sclater, Jennifer, Fiore Sicoly, Philip C. Abrami, and C. Anne Wade. 2006. "Ubiquitous Technology Integration in Canadian Public Schools: Year One Study." *Canadian Journal of Learning and Technology* 32.

Scott, Jacqueline. 2004. "Family, Gender, and Educational Attainment in Britain: A Longitudinal Study." *Journal of Comparative Family Studies* 35:565–89.

Thiessen, Victor. 2008. "Acquiring Literacy Skills: A Comparison of Provincial and International Results from PISA and IALSS." Toronto: Council of Ministers of Education in Canada.

Thiessen, Victor and E. Dianne Looker. 2006. "Do New Communication Technologies Maintain or Erode Cultural Identity? The Experiences of Canadian Youth in Northern Communities, Indian Reserves, and among African Canadians." Paper presented at the International Sociological Association Meetings, July 27, Durban, SA.

———. 2007. "Digital Divides and Capital Conversion." *Information, Communication and Society* 10:159–80.

———. 2008. "Cultural Centrality and Information and Communication Technology among Canadian Youth." *Canadian Journal of Sociology* 33(2):311–36.

U.S. Department of Commerce. 2000. "Falling Through the Net: Toward Digital Inclusion." Vol. 2003. Washington, DC: U.S. Department of Commerce and National Telecommunications and Information Administration.

van Dijk, Jan A.G.M. 2006. "Digital Divide Research, Achievements and Shortcomings." *Poetics* 34:221–35.

Van Dijk, Jan A.G.M. and Kenneth Hacker. 2003. "The Digital Divide as a Complex and Dynamic Phenomenon." *The Information Society* 19:315–26.

Vandenberghe, Christine N. and Mark J. Gierl. 2001. "Differential Bundle Functioning on Three Achievement Tests: A Comparison of Aboriginal and Non-aboriginal Examinees." Paper presented at the annual meeting of the *American Educational Research Association*, Seattle, WA. 10–14 April.

Volman, Monique and Edith van Eck. 2001. "Gender Equity and Information Technology in Education: The Second Decade." *Review of Educational Research* 71:613–34.

Volman, Monique, Edith van Eck, Irma Heemskerk, and Els Kuiper. 2005. "New Technologies, New Differences. Gender and Ethnic Differences in Pupils' Use of ICT in Primary and Secondary Education." *Computers & Education* 45:35–55.

Wasserman, Ira M. and Marie Richmond-Abbott. 2005. "Gender and the Internet: Causes of Variation in Access, Level, and Scope of Use." *Social Science Quarterly* 86:252–70.

Wenglinsky, Harold. 2003. "Using Large-scale Research to Gauge the Impact of Instructional Practices on Student Reading Comprehension: An Exploratory Study." *Education Policy Analysis Archives* 11. http://epaa.asu.edu/epaa/v11n19/.

Chapter 4

Gendered technologies as divide, diversity, and distraction

Brian Lewis Campbell

Alyssa Henning

In this study of adolescents in Nunavut and Nova Scotia we analyze a range of gendered differences and similarities in information and communication technology (ICT) access, types of computer use, and computer skills. We show that although there are gender differences in ICT skills and use, this does not translate into a simple gendered digital divide. ICT use is gendered, but the digital advantage is sometimes in favour of males and sometimes in favour of females. Any consideration of a digital divide must be seen in the context of this digital diversity. An essential component of the digital divide is a distinction between those who have and those who have not, and there are such divides revealed in our data. One of the gendered patterns of computer use that we discover, however, is a digital distraction, where some young people suffer negative consequences from the apparent overuse of some technologies. A more comprehensive conceptualization of the digital divide should include a distinction between those who can control and contextualize technology versus those who are diverted from other important goals through technology use as a distraction.

The literature documents ICT access, patterns of use, and skills as highly gendered. Early studies of access to computers and technology show large gender differences. For instance, Fife-Schaw et al. (1986) studied teenage computer usage and found that 61.7% of males reported having a computer at home, while only 39% of females made this same claim. The authors argued that the gender gap may be even greater than these figures, because it was not asked if the home-based computer was the respondent's own. Bannert and Arbinger (1996) conducted a study of students in grades five through ten in Rhineland-Palatine schools and found gender differences in relation to access to computers. In all grade levels studied, boys owned a computer more often than girls in that same grade level. Overall, 76% of all boys had possession of their own computer, whereas only 44% of all girls reported owning a computer. Bannert and Arbinger argue that "girls are indeed 'disadvantaged' in reference to their exposure to computers" (278). On the other hand, Colley and Comber (2003), who compared eleven- to twelve-year-old students and fifteen- to sixteen-year-old students, found no significant gender differences in access to a home personal computer in either age bracket. Results indicated a significant difference in access to a games computer/ console at home, with boys having much higher ownership rates than girls. For instance, 82% of eleven- and twelve-year-old boys owned a game computer/ console, compared to only 54% of eleven- and twelve-year-old girls. Similarly, 70% of fifteen- and sixteen-year-old boys owned a home game computer/ console compared to only 50% of girls (Colley and Comber 2003).

Some studies have concluded that, on average, boys spend more time on computers than girls. Bannert and Arbinger (1996) found that elementary-school-aged boys use the computer, on average, for one and half hours per day, while girls use the computer less than one hour per day. Likewise, Ching, Basham, and Jang (2005) reported that among university students, males reported higher frequency of use than female students. Other studies have argued that recently there has emerged a more subtle set of gendered ICT differences among young people. Durndell and Thomson (1997) examined more closely the computer being used and found that, although males report higher levels of use on their own computer and on a friend's computer, there were no significant gender differences in terms of use on a family or school computer. Other studies report that, while there were no significant differences in the time frame of each computer use between males and females, boys use the computer more times per week than girls (Harris 1999; Miller, Schweingruber, and Brandenburg 2001). Although the time frame spent on computers was found to be roughly equal, boys are termed "frequent users," while females are termed "occasional users" (Harris, 1999, 334).

Many studies also conclude that boys tend to spend longer periods online than females. Kraut et al. (1999) concluded that male teens spend the most hours online per week, followed by female teens, then adult males, and lastly adult females. Likewise, Odell et al. (2000) found that males spend, on average, 7.1 hours per week online, while females spend 5.4 hours per week online.

A major observation in the literature is the gendered nature of computer gaming and communication. It is often argued that males use the computer for entertainment and leisure purposes, while females use the computer for pragmatic or social purposes (Singh 2001; Weiser 2000). Jackson et al. (2001) created and tested a model of computer usage in which Internet use is generally influenced by cognitive, motivational, and affective factors. In this study, females were found to communicate through email more than males, thus signifying their stronger motives for interpersonal communication. This is consistent with Weiser's (2000) finding that females use the computer for social purposes. Males, on the other hand, had a stronger motivation for knowledge and information and were found to search the web more frequently than females (Jackson et al. 2001). Jackson et al. (2001) also argued that females may use email as a means to cope when they experience depression and loneliness.

Males are more likely than females to play or prefer to play computer/ Internet games (Colley and Comber 2003; Harris 1999; Joiner et al. 2005; Kafai and Sutton 1999; Kent and Facer 2004; Lenhart, Rainie, and Lewis 2001; Mumtaz 2001, Odell et al. 2000; Papastergiou and Solomonidou 2005; Stewart and Choi 2003; Subrahmanyam et al. 2001; Weiser, 2000). For instance, Kent and Facer (2004) found that 83% of boys played computer games at least weekly, compared to 68% of girls. Likewise, Lenhart et al. (2001) states that 75% of boys in their sample played or have downloaded a game, while only 57% of girls reported doing so. Papastergio and Solomonidou (2005) reported that 9% of boys state they have never played a game, compared to 25% of females. Gross (2004) found a small group of students who were deemed "heavy gamers," and approximately 86% of this group was male. Some studies show that females are also playing computer games; for instance, Miller et al. (2001) discovered that the number one use of the computer for both genders in their study was playing games. There was no significant difference between the males who chose games as the number one use and the females who chose this answer. Likewise, Durndell, Glissov, and Siann (1995) found that both boys and girls used computer games at school equally.

Research on Internet communication tends to show gender differences as well. Various researchers have argued that females use the Internet for communication at higher rates than males, or at least prefer to use email more (Czerniewicz and Ng'ambi 2004; Jackson et al. 2001; Kraut et al. 1999; Leung 2001; Miller et al. 2001, Mumtaz 2001; Odell et al. 2000; Subrahmanyam et al. 2001; Weiser 2000). For instance, Czerniewicz and Ng'ambi (2004) discovered that 75% of those participating in computer communication were female. In their study, Miller et al. (2001) found that 48% of girls used a home computer for email, while only 38% of boys reported doing so. In a similar study of university and college students, 91% of females used the Internet for email, while 86% of boys reported this use (Odell et al. 2000). As with gaming, there are studies that show no differences between males and females in computer use for communication purposes. Papastergiou and Solomonidou (2005) found no gender differences in communication techniques, including emailing other pupils, emailing other persons, chat with other pupils, and chat with other persons. Likewise, Joiner et al. (2005) found no significant gender differences in terms of online communication. Losh (2004) looked at email use ownership longitudinally and discovered that males had more email in 1997, but by 2002 females reported slightly more ownership.

Smith and Necessary (1996) studied the effect of computer experience on computer skills and found a significant relationship. Students who had more experience with computers also had higher computer literacy. This phenomenon was gendered in that boys had more experience with computers and higher skills, while females had less experience and lower skills. These patterns were also discovered in Ilomaki and Rantanen's (2007) study of secondary students. A select group of students were given laptops to use at school and at home over a three-year period. Tests of computer literacy were given throughout this study, and by the end of the three years, students were showing great improvements in computer literacy. The authors argued that both female and male students had the basic computer knowledge by the end of the study and could now function in the current computer-knowledge society.

One must be careful with conclusions about computer skills, because researchers often use different mechanisms to study computer skills. Some researchers examine the confidence levels of respondents (see, for example, Durndell and Haag 2002; Harrison, Rainer, and Hochwarter 1997; Young 2000), while others ask respondents to rate themselves (see, for example, Herskovic et al. 2000; Li and Kirkup 2007; Messineo and DeOllos 2005). Studies of confidence levels are not a great measure of skill and can be more closely related to the attitudes of respondents toward computers. Advanced studies actually test out the skill levels of the population; however, these studies are rare (see, for example, Durndell 1991; Durndell and Thomson 1997; Ilomaki and Rantanen 2007; Lee 2003).

Most studies find that males report higher computer skills or computer confidence (Durndell and Haag 2002; Durndell and Thomson 1997; Harrison et al. 1997; Herskovic et al. 2000; Houtz and Gupta 2001; Lee 2003; Messineo and DeOllos 2005; Smith and Necessary 1996; Van Dijk and Hacker 2003). For instance, 17% of males and only 6% of females stated they had "good skills" in a Dutch study (Van Dijk and Hacker 2003). Similarly, Durndell and Thomson (1997) conducted a test of computer performance and found that males consistently had higher skills.

Some studies report that males do outscore females on some skills; however, there is gender equality on other skills. For instance, Herskovic et al. (2000) found higher male ratings in email use and Medline searching and slightly higher ratings in spreadsheet use. On the other hand, the ratings for word processing were gender equal. Other studies have reported that males and females have equal computer skills (Rajagopal and Bojin 2003; Young 2000). Volman et al. (2005) also reported that differences among female and males are minimal at both the primary and secondary education levels in the Netherlands.

Overall, the literature on adolescent computing, in many cases, shows gendered ICT access, use, and skills. In some cases, recent research shows that despite aspects of convergence there is persistence in computing as a gendered activity.

Below we examine the case of computing access, use, and skills in relation to high-school-aged adolescents in Nunavut and Nova Scotia. These issues are explored using the surveys of high school students in Nunavut and Nova Scotia that were conducted as part of the Equity and Technology project. In discussing our findings, we analyze the Nova Scotia and the Nunavut data separately, since the differences between north and south are often far greater than gender differences.

ACCESS TO COMPUTERS

Our data show mostly small gendered differences in access to computers. In Nova Scotia only 4% of females and 4% of males did not have a computer at home. Nova Scotia males were slightly more likely to claim to have more computers than females with 24% claiming three or more as compared to 20% of females. In Nunavut, overall computer access is lower, showing a pattern of greater gender differences with 38% of males and 42% of females claiming no computer at home. At the high end, 11% of Nunavut males claim to have three or more computers at home as compared to only 5% for females. Of course, having computers in the home does not guarantee access to these computers.

When we considered access to home computers we looked at the difference between accessing the respondent's own computer and accessing their family's computer. In Nova Scotia males are more likely to use their own computer, with 24% accessing only their own computer over the last week compared to 21% of females. Slightly more Nova Scotia males than females, 44% compared to 38%, used both their own and their family's computer over the last week, while 35% of females compared to 25% of males accessed only their family's computer over the last week. Males are more likely to claim access to their own computer while females are more likely to claim access to their family's computer. The Nunavut responses do not show the same level of gendered patterns. For both males and females, 11% used their own computer. Females are slightly more likely to claim only using the family's computer, 23% compared to 18%.

Using friends' computers, school computers, and other public access computers over the last week have different gendered patterns in both Nunavut and in Nova Scotia. In Nunavut, females are slightly more likely to use a school computer (77% compared to 74%) or another public access computer (44% compared to 37%) and males are more likely to have used a friend's computer (38% compared to 30%). In Nova Scotia, males are more likely to claim use over the last week on all of these types of computers.

Internet connectivity does not vary greatly by gender in the south or the north. Men claim slightly higher levels of connectivity in all cases, which is in line with their claim for slightly higher numbers of computers. When we looked at the proportion of these computers that are connected to the Internet we saw virtually identical relationships. For example, in Nova Scotia 6% of males and 5% of females do not have home computers that are connected to the Internet. In Nunavut, the lack of connection is far higher, with 50% of males and 51% of females not having any home computer connected to the Internet. The large differences in connectivity are between Nunavut and Nova Scotia and not between genders.

There is a far greater reliance on public access computing for all adolescents in Nunavut than in Nova Scotia. This greater reliance on public computing in Nunavut can be clearly seen in respondents' answers to the question "Which one place do you use the Internet the most?" In Nunavut, 32% of males and 26% of females indicated that home is the place most used for Internet access. This compares with 86% for males and 85% for females in Nova Scotia. School computers are by far the most likely place for Nunavut youth to access the Internet, as indicated by 53% of females and 53% of males. In Nova Scotia only 8% of males and 8% of females indicated the same. There are slight gender differences in access patterns, but the main differences are regional.

Although there are some gendered patterns in access to computing, most of these differences are small. There is little evidence of a gendered digital access divide. Overall, Nova Scotia male adolescents claim a slightly higher level of access when compared to Nova Scotia female adolescents. In Nunavut, the picture is more mixed, with females sometimes showing higher levels of access than males, and there is a far greater reliance on public access computers overall.

PATTERNS OF USE

The slight access advantage for Nova Scotia males is paralleled by a slightly higher level of ICT use. When we look at time spent on the Internet, Nova Scotia males claim slightly higher amounts of time on their home computer with 19% claiming over fifteen hours per week as compared to 13% for Nova Scotia females. Females are slightly higher than males in the six- to fifteen-hour categories and are the same as males in the groups tallying five hours or less. There are also slightly higher levels of use of school computers for Nova Scotia males. In Nunavut the use of school computers for Internet access is equal for males and females, and males again report a slightly higher level of use of home computers for Internet access than females. Both females and males appear to use the Internet more at school in Nunavut, and at home in Nova Scotia.

This slightly higher level of male use does not, however, become in any simple way an ICT advantage. Patterns of ICT use are gendered, but the pattern is one where females are much more likely to have higher levels in some areas than males. There are different sets of gendered strengths in ICT. Female respondents claim higher levels of activity in communication-related

TABLE 4.1

Most common use of the Internet by gender for Nunavut and Nova Scotia

	Nunavut		Nova Scotia	
What do you use the Internet for the most?	Male (%)	Female (%)	Male (%)	Female (%)
To do school work	21	25	20**	27**
To exchange emails with people	27**	51**	7**	11**
For games	34**	13**	21**	5**
For job-related activities	3	2	2	1
For instant messaging	25*	33*	51**	68**
Other	12**	4 **	13**	8**

The base of percentages for Nova Scotia was 1044 (females) and 816 (males).

The base of percentages for Nunavut was 282 (females) and 293 (males).

Note: Some students choose more than one answer, making this a multiple-response table.

*p<0.05; **p<0.01.

computer use, while males tend to claim higher levels of activity in technical and gaming aspects of computer use. Table 4.1 displays the most common use of the Internet by gender for youth in Nunavut and Nova Scotia.

It is interesting that the percentage of youth reporting using the Internet "to do school work" is very similar in both the north and the south, with females slightly higher and at similar levels in both locations (although it is statistically insignificant in Nunavut). The most gendered areas of ICT are communications and gaming. A sizable minority of males have gaming as their primary use of the Internet in both locations. In Nunavut, 34% of males, and in Nova Scotia, 21% of males cite gaming as their most common Internet use. In contrast, only 13% of females in Nunavut have gaming as their most common Internet use, and in Nova Scotia this is only 5%. In the more highly connected south there is a lower level of Internet gaming overall. Females in Nunavut are nearly twice as likely as males to have email as their most common Internet activity at 51% compared to 27% for males. Email use is much lower in the highly connected south in favour of synchronous communication, with 68% of females and 51% of males indicating instant messaging as their most common use of the Internet. In both the north and the south, interpersonal communication is the most important use. There is little difference between Nunavut and Nova Scotia, with females select-ing communication (whether asynchronous or synchronous) as the most important Internet use. If we combine email and instant messaging, 84% of females in Nunavut and 79% in Nova Scotia claim interpersonal communication as their most common form of Internet use. For males the corresponding figures are 52% and 58%. Although it was also the most important use for males in both the south and the north, females were over 20% higher on interpersonal communication as their most common use of the Internet in both locations.

Table 4.2 shows the percentage of respondents who have used various interpersonal communications technologies at least a few times a week. The email items are broken out by the audience for the communication. Very few respondents of either gender email teachers regularly. Only 14% of males and 8% of females frequently correspond through email with teachers. In Nunavut most males and females, 77% and 70% respectively, never email a teacher, while the corresponding figures in Nova Scotia are 54% and 59% (figures not shown in table). Classmates have a higher priority than teachers for email with many students. In the south, although just over a third of respondents claim never to email classmates, both females (26%) and males (27%) email classmates at least a few times a week. The pattern in Nunavut is more gendered with 47% of females emailing classmates at least a few times a week compared to 34% for males.

TABLE 4.2

Interpersonal communication technology use of at least a few times a week by gender for Nunavut and Nova Scotia

Communication technology	Nunavut		Nova Scotia	
	Male (%)	Female (%)	Male (%)	Female (%)
Email teachers	9	10	14**	8**
Email classmates	34**	47**	27	26
Email friends	51**	72**	43**	55**
Email family	26**	50**	24	24
Instant messaging	48	48	81**	85**
Text messaging	28	27	51	50

The base of percentages for Nova Scotia ranged from 1044 to 1048 (females) and 820 to 824 (males).

The base of percentages for Nunavut ranged from 269 to 272 (females) and 277 to 282 (males).

Note: Each response to communication technology refers to the number/percentage of students who use the communication technology at least a few times each week (which includes a few times a week, almost every day and once a day or more).

*p<0.05; **p<0.01.

This higher level of email activity with classmates in the north can perhaps be explained by the higher reliance on email as opposed to instant messaging and a higher degree of overlap between classmates and friends. Emailing with friends is gendered in both the north and the south, with females using email with friends to a greater extent than males. In Nunavut, 72% of females email their friends at least a few times a week as compared to 51% of males. In the south the reliance on email is lower, but here, too, it is also gendered, with 55% of females emailing friends at least a few times a week compared to 43% of males. Unfortunately the questionnaire did not break down the audiences for instant messaging. Given the young profile of users of this medium it is probably safe to say that the main audience is friends. Instant messaging is gendered in Nova Scotia, with female respondents claiming slightly higher levels of use; 85% report that they use it at least a few times a week compared with 81% for males. At the other end of the spectrum, 10% of males, compared with 5% of females, indicate that they never use instant messaging. The Nunavut data show no gender relationship on far lower levels of instant messaging. Overall, email and instant messaging show females at least the same as or higher than males. This is especially clear in relation to peer communication.

Beyond the focus on peers, the female strengths in the use of interpersonal communication extend to family. In Nova Scotia, although at the high-user end, both female and male respondents are fairly equal in emailing family, with 24% and 24% respectively indicating at least a few times each week. Cumulatively, however, female respondents are slightly more likely to email family; only 29% of females, compared to 39% of males indicate they never email family. In Nunavut the female focus on family communications is much stronger than their male counterparts, with 50% emailing family at least a few times a week compared with 26% for males.

TABLE 4.3

Website and web log use creation by gender for Nunavut and Nova Scotia

	Nunavut		Nova Scotia	
	Male (%)	Female (%)	Male (%)	Female (%)
Website	8	9	25**	44**
Web log	7	9	17**	26**

The base of percentages for Nova Scotia ranged from 1035 to 1050 (females) and 824 to 837 (males).

The base of percentages for Nunavut was 270 to 277 (females) and 286 to 287 (males).

*p<0.05; **p<0.01.

The strength of females in communications technology is further demonstrated when we consider the creation of websites and web logs or blogs. In Table 4.3 we can see that there are few young people in the north with either their own website or their own web log, and there is very little difference between genders. In the south, however, females are much more likely than males to have either websites or web logs. Females' strength in the use of ICT goes beyond interpersonal communication to more general forms of online expression.

Many males are more interested in computer gaming than other computer uses. Above, we outlined the much greater likelihood that males will cite gaming as their primary use of the Internet (see Table 4.1). In Table 4.4 we summarize the findings from two additional game-focused questions. We asked respondents to agree or disagree with the statement "when I use the computer it is mostly to play games," and we asked about the amount of time spent playing games. In both Nunavut and Nova Scotia, males are much more likely to state that playing games was one of their primary uses of the computer. In the south, 34% of males compared to 14% of females agree that playing computer games is one of their primary computer uses. In Nunavut these values are higher overall, with the same gendered trend of 46% for males and 28% for females. Males also are more likely to state that they play computer games at least a few times a week. This difference is greater in the south, with much lower gaming values for females.

We further explored gendered differences in computer use with statistical segmentation techniques. We did a CHAID[1] analysis, in which we looked for the most important gender differentiator in computer application

TABLE 4.4

Game orientation and frequency by gender for Nunavut and Nova Scotia

	Nunavut		Nova Scotia	
	Male (%)	Female (%)	Male (%)	Female (%)
Agree or Strongly Agree with "When I use the computer it is mostly to play games"	46**	28**	34**	14**
Play computer games at least a few times each week	65**	53**	57**	35**

The base of percentages for Nova Scotia ranged from 1041 to 1049 (females) and 819 to 824 (males).

The base of percentages for Nunavut was 271 to 272 (females) and 277 to 281 (males).

*p<0.05; **p<0.01.

use. The main differentiator was computer gaming with a second differentiator being communication. With gaming and communication marked out as the most statistically significant differentiators, we looked for any underlying groups who might vary on these issues. We examined a series of gaming and communication variables. In relation to gaming, we looked at whether the primary use of the Internet was gaming, whether the primary use of the computer was to play games, and the frequency of playing computer games. In relation to communications we looked at the frequency of instant messaging, the frequency of emailing friends, and the frequency of emailing family. We did a Latent Class Cluster analysis[2] with these variables and came up with four types of computer users in relation to communicating and gaming: those respondents who are low on both (Low Communicator-Gamers), those who are relatively high on all uses (High Communicator-Gamers), those who are high on communications and low on gaming (Communicators), and those who are low on communication and high on gaming (Gamers). These four groups emerged in both the Nova Scotia and the Nunavut analyses. Table 4.5 shows the gender breakdowns for these four groups in both Nova Scotia and in Nunavut.[3]

Females in both populations are more likely to be Low Communicator-Gamers and Communicators. Males are more likely to be High Communicator-Gamers and Gamers.

There is a gendered digital diversity when we look at gaming and communication. When we look at patterns of computer use we see a division between males, who are interested in gaming, and females, who are interested

TABLE 4.5

Technology use cluster groups by gender for Nunavut and Nova Scotia

Technology use cluster group	Gender and location			
	Nova Scotia females	Nova Scotia males	Nunavut females	Nunavut males
Low communicator-gamers (%)	68	57	40	33
Communicators (%)	22	15	30	13
High communicator-gamers (%)	8	20	9	18
Gamers (%)	1	8	20	36
Total (%)	100	100	100	100
Ns	1011	784	266	272

in communication. The higher levels of communication computing for females goes beyond email and instant messaging to higher levels of website and web log creation. There is some indication that males have higher levels of computing activity overall.

SKILLS

Since females claim to be more active in their use of Internet communication technologies, it is reasonable to assume that this will be reflected in their self-assessment of skill. Table 4.6 summarizes the self-assessment of skill by respondents on a range of computer-related tasks. Respondents were asked to rate themselves on a four-point scale that was labelled "I don't know how to do this," "I can do this but I sometimes need help," "I can do this without help," and "I can teach others how to do this." The table combines the top two levels of skill assessment into a high-skill category. The accessibility and level-of-use differences between Nunavut and Nova Scotia outlined above are reflected in these skill patterns, with much higher overall levels of skill self-assessment reported in the south. In both Nunavut and Nova Scotia most skills show little gender difference. Cut, copy, and paste skills, for example, are claimed by 46% of males and 46% of females in Nunavut, with corresponding values of 95% and 98% in Nova Scotia. Females in the south are higher in web-page creation skills, with 67% (compared to 60% for males) claiming high skill for creating web pages with words and 65% claiming high skill when web pages include words and pictures (compared to 59% for males). This result is reversed in Nunavut. The only areas in which females in Nunavut claim higher skills than males are in text formatting (81% compared to 74%) and in spell checking (69% compared to 63%). In Nova Scotia, males claim higher levels of skill in mathematical functions (47% compared to 26%) and in spreadsheet graphics (51% compared to 39%). Males in Nova Scotia also claim higher levels of skill in page-break creation, professional looking documents, and putting sounds into computer presentations.

If we look at these skill claims overall, males are slightly more likely to make high-skills claims in Nova Scotia, with an average of 79% compared to 76% for females. In Nunavut, males clearly claim higher skills, with an average of 42% compared to 38% for females.

We must be cautious in our interpretation of skill claims. Males express slightly more confidence than females in their skills, but we must keep in mind that this is not an actual test of skills. In Table 4.7 we show one aspect of the

TABLE 4.6

Computer and Internet high-level skills by gender for Nunavut and Nova Scotia

	Nunavut		Nova Scotia	
	Male (%)	Female (%)	Male (%)	Female (%)
Cut, copy, and paste	46	46	95**	98**
Choose printing options (i.e., paper size and orientation, number of copies)	55	51	83	84
Making folders	53	53	89	87
Change settings on the Control Panel (such as date, time, sound, and monitor setting)	48**	37**	88	85
Choose font size, type of text, and bold, italic, and underline	74*	81*	96**	98**
Make section and page breaks in a document	28	23	66**	56**
Use spell check	63	69	93**	97**
Make a professional looking document that includes text, graphics, and charts	25	18	70**	61**
Use math functions such as sum, average, max, min, count in spreadsheet	30**	19**	47**	26**
Make charts or graphs in a spreadsheet	34*	26*	51**	39**
Search the Internet using a search engine (such as Google or Yahoo!)	84	83	97**	99**
Send an attachment with an email	53	53	86*	89*
Copy or download files from the Internet	55*	46*	90	89
Make a web page that has words	22*	14*	60**	67**
Make a web page that has words and pictures	21	16	59**	65**
Bookmark a website	31**	20**	87**	81**
Make a computer presentation using a program like PowerPoint	24	17	85	83
Put sounds into a computer presentation like PowerPoint	20**	11**	76**	68**
Edit pictures and photos on the computer	40	35	78	76
Total Average Percentage of High-skill Claims	42	38	79	76

The base of percentages for Nova Scotia ranged from 1044–1055 (females), and 825–835 (males).

The base of percentages for Nunavut ranged from 270–278 (females) and 272–283 (males).

Note: Each response to refers to the percentage of students who describe their ability to use the particular computer or Internet function at a high skill level, which includes "I can do this without help" and "I can teach others how to do this."

*p<0.05; **p<0.01.

TABLE 4.7

Confidence in ability to create web pages by actual web-page creation
and gender for Nova Scotia

Gender	Own a web page	How well can you make a web page that has words and pictures?			
		I don't know how to do this	I can do this but sometimes I need help	I can do this without help	I can teach others how to do this
Male Ns	N/A	198	139	170	315
Males (%)	Yes	4	7	19	50
	No	96	94	81	51
	Total	100	100	100	100
Females (%)	Yes	2	22	39	73
	No	99	78	61	28
	Total	100	100	100	100
Female Ns	N/A	197	164	216	459

Note: Any errors in percentages are due to rounding.

relationship between the self-assessment of skill and practice. We look at the
skill claims in making web pages using both words and pictures and then compare these claims to the self-reported actual practice of males and females in
website creation. It is interesting that 51% of males who assess themselves
highly on web-page creation skills do not have their own web page. This compares to 28% of females. A similar gap occurs at the "I can do this without
help" level, where 81% of males who claim this level of skill do not have a web
page, compared to 61% of females. This pattern is repeated in Nunavut (not
shown), although the very small numbers (due to a lack of personal web pages)
make the percentages less stable.

Male confidence can also be seen when respondents were asked to rate
themselves and others on a seven-point scale, from 1 being no ability to 7
being expert ability. Table 4.8 displays the mean scores for these ratings. It is
interesting that both males and females rate themselves more highly skilled compared to most others. On average, males and females in both the north and
south assess their most computer-skilled teacher as more highly skilled than
themselves. Their closest friends are also rated higher with the exception of
Nova Scotia males who rate them slightly lower. In Nunavut, females' self-
rating average score is slightly higher than their average score for female

TABLE 4.8

Mean self-rating of skill level by gender for Nunavut and Nova Scotia

On a scale of 1 (no ability) to 7 (expert ability) rate:	Nunavut		Nova Scotia	
	Male	Female	Male	Female
Yourself	4.16	4.15	5.36	5.19
Your Father	4.05	3.85	3.60	3.86
Your Mother	3.81	3.76	3.45	3.59
Your most computer skilled teacher	5.55	5.84	6.07	6.15
Your least computer skilled teacher	3.45	3.53	2.63	2.74
Your closest friends	4.32	4.43	5.28	5.30
Your male classmates	4.01	4.01	4.86	5.05
Your female classmates	3.82	4.43	4.48	5.01

The base of means for Nova Scotia ranged from 956–1051 (females), and 790–832 (males).

The base of means for Nunavut ranged from 240–271 (females) and 257–282 (males).

classmates, and in Nova Scotia females' average score is very close to that given by females for their female classmates. Males, however, discount female classmates both in the north and in the south. The differential in the north (4.16 compared to 3.82), is not as wide as it is in the south, where males rate themselves 5.36 and females 4.48). Male confidence seems to be paired with a discount for female skill.

When we consider skills overall, we see mostly small aggregate differences between males and females. The differences are larger in the north than in the south. In the south, females claim higher levels of skill in areas connected to communication than do males. There is also some indication that males may be more likely to express confidence in their own skills in areas where they do not have as much experience as females. Males who are confident enough to claim that they can teach others how to create web pages are less likely to have their own web page than females who make similar claims. Males also discount the average skills of female students, while females tend not to discount the average skills of their male colleagues. Despite these overall aggregate differences, the main finding is that males and females have different average strengths in computing and in gaming. Males are more likely to claim higher levels of use in math and computational uses of computers.

ACADEMIC CONSEQUENCES

In considering the impact of the gendered skills outlined above we will look at the self-reported grades of these high school students. We show that there are gendered academic consequences of digital time use and skill.

Table 4.9 displays a percentage breakdown for Nova Scotia by gender and grade averages (80% or above and below 80%) of those students who claimed "I can teach others how to do this" for a number of computer skills. Having high computer skills is often related to having higher grades for both males and females. This is true of education-related computer skills (such as creating a professional looking document and PowerPoint presentations) and more general computer skills (such as bookmarking websites and using an Internet search engine). For instance, 68% of females with high grades report being able to bookmark a website, compared with 55.7% of females with lower grades. The same pattern appears for males, where 82% of males with high grades report being able to bookmark a website, compared with 63% of males with lower grades.

Interestingly, two computer skills had the opposite pattern for females. Females who claim to have high skills in creating a website with words and creating a website with words and pictures are more likely to have lower grades. Forty-two percent of females with high grades claim they are able to teach others how to create a website with words and pictures, compared with 51% of females with lower grades making this same claim. This trend was not seen in males for any skills. Being competent in website skills may be seen as a distraction for females.

More computer skill differences were statistically significant by grades for males than for females in Nova Scotia. Specifically, seventeen computer skills are related to male grades, and only nine computer skills are significantly related to female grades. Males' grades are correlated with more computer skills than females' grades, specifically with making folders, changing computer settings, creating page breaks, spreadsheet math functions, spreadsheet chart/graph functions, downloading files, creating a PowerPoint presentation, putting sounds in PowerPoint, and editing pictures.

Since the overall level of computer skills is lower in Nunavut, we have combined the top two levels of "I can do this without help" and "I can teach others how to do this" categories for our high-skill category in Table 4.10. In Nunavut, the same trends emerge for males, with higher computer skills seen in males with higher grades. For instance, 51% of Nunavut males with grades

TABLE 4.9
High computer and Internet skills by grades and gender for Nova Scotia

High computer and Internet skill	Average grade			
	Percentage of females under 80%	Percentage of females 80% and over	Percentage of males under 80%	Percentage of males 80% and over
Cutting and pasting	82**	91**	79**	88**
Print options	46**	56**	48**	60**
Making folders	65	70	68**	77**
Computer settings	58	59	63*	70*
Font properties	83**	93**	80**	91**
Page breaks in documents	27	30	34**	46**
Spell-check	77**	88**	72**	87**
Create professional-looking documents	29*	36*	36**	50**
Spreadsheet math functions	9	10	18**	29**
Spreadsheet chart/graph functions	13	16	22**	31**
Internet search engine	85**	92**	81**	88**
Email attachment	69**	77**	63**	77**
Download files from the Internet	64	66	67**	77**
Web page with words	49*	42*	38	40
Web page with words and pictures	51**	42**	38	39
Bookmark websites	56**	68**	63**	82**
Create a PowerPoint presentation	57	62	58**	69**
Put sounds in PowerPoint	45	44	50**	64**
Edit pictures	53	50	50*	57*
Average (%)	54	57	54	64

The base of percentages for Nova Scotia ranged from 366 to 373 (females <80), 608 to 614 (females >80), 425 to 432 (males <80), and 338 to 432 (males >80).

Each response refers to the percentage of students who describe their ability to use the particular computer or Internet function as "I can teach others how to do this."

*p<0.05; **p<0.01.

TABLE 4.10

High computer and Internet skills by grades for Nunavut

High computer and Internet skill	Average grade			
	Percentage of females under 80%	Percentage of females 80% and over	Percentage of males under 80%	Percentage of males 80% and over
Cutting and pasting	53	48	50	50
Print options	56	50	51**	74**
Making folders	63	56	55	64
Computer settings	37	39	47	59
Font properties	83	89	74	84
Page breaks in documents	27	29	29	38
Spell-check	74	74	63	71
Create professional-looking documents	23	21	24*	38*
Spreadsheet math functions	24	20	30	38
Spreadsheet chart/graph functions	31	27	35*	49*
Internet search engine	86	91	84	92
Email attachment	52	64	54	67
Download files from the Internet	45*	61*	55	65
Web page with words	15	19	23	30
Web page with words and pictures	16	21	20*	32*
Bookmark websites	21	26	34	40
Create a PowerPoint presentation	19	21	27	32
Put sounds in PowerPoint	13	11	19	29
Edit pictures	35	43	41*	59*
Average (%)	41	43	43	53

The base of percentages for Nunavut ranged from 114 to 119 (females <80), 68 to 70 (females >80), 143 to 139 (males <80), and 64 to 61 (males >80).

Each response refers to the percentage of students who describe their ability to use the particular computer or Internet function as "I can do this without help" or "I can teach others how to do this."

*p<0.05; **p<0.01.

under 80% claim to have high print-option skills, compared with 74% of Nunavut males with grades of 80% and over. The same pattern appears for creating professional looking documents, spreadsheet chart/graph functions, creating a web page with words and pictures, and editing pictures. For females the only significant pattern emerged with downloading Internet files, with only 45% of Nunavut females with grades under 80% stating they have high skills, compared with 61% of Nunavut females with grades of 80% and above. Again, computer skills are positively related to male grades more than female grades, with five computer skills influencing grades for Nunavut males and only one skill being related to the grades of Nunavut females. This is also true when examining average skill ratings. There is only a slight difference in average skill ratings for females with high grades compared to females with low grades. However, males with high grades have an average skill rating of 53%, and males with low grades have an average skill rating of 43%. This overall pattern of high levels of self-reported skill among males with higher grades is consistent with that found in Nova Scotia.

When we look at some measures of the relationship between grades and computer skills and use in females we see a reversal of the positive association seen for males. In Table 4.11 we show the top self-rating for overall computer skills, where respondents rated themselves on a seven-point scale from 1 for no ability to 7 for expert ability. This table shows respondents who rated themselves as a 6 or higher. Table 4.12 shows the same data for Nunavut. In both the Nova Scotia and Nunavut cases, males with higher grades have higher self-assessments of computer skill. Only males with higher averages have higher computer skill ratings in Nunavut, while males overall have higher skill assessments in Nova Scotia. Interestingly though, in Nova Scotia, females with lower grades rate their overall computer skills more highly than females with higher

TABLE 4.11

High self-rating of computer skills by grades in Nova Scotia

Rating	Females: Under 80%	Females: 80% and over	Males: Under 80%	Males: 80% and over
Ns	373	613	431	342
6 or higher (%)	38*	31*	43	48

Response refers to the percentage of students who rate their computer skills as either 6 or 7 on a seven-point scale.
*p<0.05.

TABLE 4.12

High self-rating of computer skills by grades in Nunavut

Rating	Females: Under 80%	Females: 80% and over	Males: Under 80%	Males: 80% and over
Ns	119	69	146	64
6 or higher (%)	13	15	14*	28*

Response refers to the percentage of students who rate their computer skills as either 6 or 7 on a seven-point scale.
*p<0.05.

grades. When we analyzed the source of this reversal of the male pattern, the importance of communications became apparent.

Table 4.13 shows high computer use (at least weekly), by grades, for various computer and Internet programs. Females with lower grades have higher levels of use. For instance, 72% of Nova Scotia females who have grades under 80% download music at least weekly, compared with 60% of Nova Scotia females who have grades of 80% and above. This same trend appears even when the computer program being used is specifically for a class project; 15% of Nova Scotia females with grades under 80% use computer presentation programs for class, compared with only 9% of females with grades of 80% and over.

Only two computer uses emerge as significant for males, with respect to grades: using the Internet for course purposes and using the Internet for other reasons. Opposite from females, males who used these programs frequently showed higher grades. For instance, 43% of Nova Scotia males who have grades 80% or lower use the Internet for courses, compared with 52% of Nova Scotia males who have grades 80% or higher.

For females, the majority of the programs shown to be significant with respect to grades focus around interpersonal communication, such as emailing friends, family, and classmates, and text messaging. As described previously, females are more likely than males to use these programs overall, thus it is important to consider that females using these programs are showing lower grades.

In Nunavut, the only computer program that appeared to correlate with grades for females was emailing teachers. When females reported higher frequencies of emailing teachers, higher grades did emerge. Specifically, 17% of Nunavut females with grades of 80% and above reporting

TABLE 4.13

Computer use by grades and gender for Nova Scotia

High computer and Internet use	Average grade			
	Percentage of females under 80%	Percentage of females 80% and over	Percentage of males under 80%	Percentage of males 80% and over
Email family	28**	20**	24	22
E-mail friends	58*	51*	43	46
Email classmates	29*	22*	27	27
Text message	58**	45**	53	47
Play computer games	43**	30**	56	58
Educational software	11**	6**	17	13
Spreadsheets	9*	5*	14	16
Download music	72**	60**	71	72
Internet for courses	52	58	43**	52**
Internet for other reasons	82	85	83**	89**
Computer presentations for class	15**	9**	18	20

The base of percentages for Nova Scotia ranged from 367 to 373 (females <80), 604 to 613 (females >80), 424 to 432 (males <80), and 342 to 343 (males >80).

Each response refers to the percentage of students who use the technology program a few times each week, almost everyday, and once a day or more.

*$p<0.05$; **$p<0.01$.

emailing teachers at least weekly, compared with 7% of Nunavut females with grades under 80%. It is important to note, however, that these numbers were quite small, with only eight female students with low grades emailing teachers weekly and twelve female students with high grades emailing teachers weekly. No statistically significant findings on computer program use by grades emerged for Nunavut males.

Another analysis that helps to illuminate the association between gendered computer use patterns and school grades comes from our cluster analysis of gaming and communications differences. Table 4.14 shows gender by grades by cluster group for Nunavut, and Table 4.15 shows the same information for Nova Scotia. Males in Nunavut show small differences in cluster membership by grades. Nunavut males with grades lower than 80% are slightly more likely to be Communicators or Gamers, while males with higher grades are slightly more likely (25% as compared to 18%) to be High

TABLE 4.14

Communication-gaming cluster groups by grades and gender for Nunavut

	Average grade			
Technology use cluster group	Percentage of females under 80%	Percentage of females 80% and over	Percentage of males under 80%	Percentage of males 80% and over
Low Communicator-Gamers	36	48	36	38
Communicators	33	30	14	9
High Communicator-Gamers	8	9	18	25
Gamers	24	13	33	28
Total	100	100	100	100

The base of percentages for Nunavut was 115 (females <80), 69 (females >80), 143 (males <80), and 64 (males >80).

TABLE 4.15

Communication-gaming cluster groups by grades and gender for Nova Scotia

	Average grade			
Technology use cluster group	Percentage of females under 80%	Percentage of females 80% and over	Percentage of males under 80%	Percentage of males 80% and over
Low Communicator-Gamers	59	75	59	56
Communicators	27	18	15	14
High Communicator-Gamers	13	6	19	21
Gamers	2	1	8	8
Total	100	100	100	100

The base of percentages for Nova Scotia was 354 (females <80), 599 (females >80), 407 (males <80), and 333 (males >80).

Communicator-Gamers. In essence, the male students with higher grades are slightly more likely to engage in both. In Nova Scotia there is no association between grades and cluster membership for males.

The situation for females is quite different in both locations. Females with high grades are more likely to be Low Communicator-Gamers. This relative difference is more pronounced in Nova Scotia, where 75% of female students with an average of 80% or above are likely to be Low Communicator-Gamers, compared with 59% of females with lower averages. Females in Nova Scotia with lower averages are more likely to be high communicators, either in the Communicators cluster or combined with gaming in the High Communicator-Gamer cluster. In Nunavut, females with lower grades are more likely to be gamers compared to those with higher grades.

We have explored the relationship between gendered computing and grades. Depending on how we measure the relationship, male computing activities and skills have either no association or a slightly positive association with grades. Females generally have a positive relationship between grades and computer skills; however, females with lower grades tend to be high-volume online communicators and, in Nunavut, gamers. The direction of influence between computing patterns and academic performance is an open question. Is it the case that students with higher computer skills learn from this experience and are then better able to perform academically? Or is it the case that more academically successful students are more capable at computing? And in the case of female high communicators having low grades, where higher levels of certain types of computing perhaps serve as a distraction, is it a cause or consequence of lower academic performance?

DIGITAL DIVIDE, DIVERSITY, AND DISTRACTION

ICT access, use, and skills are gendered in different ways. Males claim slightly higher levels of access than females. This level of access does not however, translate evenly into higher levels of use. We have seen that there is a gendered digital diversity among high school students with respect to both computer skills and patterns of computer use. In some aspects of computer use females are equal with males, but in interpersonal communication uses of ICT females often exceed males. Female strength in Internet communications extends beyond simple interpersonal communication and into websites and blogs. Both males and females rate their own skills highly; however, males tend to discount female ICT skills while females are more generous in their overall assessment of others' skills. Thiessen (2007), using the Youth in Transition Study (YITS) data, has argued that female young people discount their mathematical and computer skills and that males overstate these same skills. In these populations, we have not found females to discount their skills, but we do have some evidence that males may over-claim theirs. The substance behind the rhetoric of male skill confidence is difficult to assess. It is instructive that many more males with confidence in their ability to create web pages do not have web pages while far more women have them. In practice, more women than men apply web-page editing skills. Whether males are more likely to develop computer skills in the abstract, and without application, or whether they are more likely to rhetorically inflate their actual skills is impossible to tell with the data at hand. Perhaps females simply acquire skills as needed. Perhaps females are less confident, or alternatively less boastful, of their computer skills. More detailed study of these dynamics is required to disentangle the relationships.

The use of interpersonal ICT is a form of social bonding. Although the role of females in maintaining family bonds in Nunavut is clearly seen in the much higher rate of email to family members, the preponderance of interpersonal communication by all of these adolescents is toward peers. Interpersonal ICT use for this population is primarily a form of peer interaction and bonding. On the surface it appears that females are especially strong in building peer bonds through the use of ICT. Males are more likely to play computer games and for a minority of male adolescents, computer gaming is a consuming activity. Perhaps ICT use accomplishes peer bonding through different routes for males and females, however. There is some evidence in the literature that computer gaming by males is a form of peer bonding. Colwell et al. (1995) found that boys tend to play strategy, sports, and shooter video games, and that those boys who play heavily are also more involved in seeing friends. Bonanno and Kommers (2005) also found that computer game playing males are interested in both challenge and social interaction while females who play games do not tend to seek social interaction through gaming. Unfortunately, our present study does not separate out types of gaming and levels of social interaction. Further research will have to address the extent to which the interpersonal communication emphasis of females and the gaming emphasis of males are both gendered forms of peer bonding.

The female strengths in computer skills make it difficult to accept a simple gendered digital divide with males playing the dominant role. Male adolescents still demonstrate more confidence than females, but it is not clear how much substance and consequence there is in this.

We must separate skills from patterns of use. Technology skills for both males and females are positively correlated with higher grades. It is only the pattern of high levels of use that has the negative association for females. There is a paradox for females in the relationship of higher levels of computer use and lower grades. Although females in this study report slightly lower access, those that do report high frequency of use, and therefore do have access, have poorer academic performance. This is opposite to the relationship we found with skills, where females with higher grades report higher levels of computer skill. Perhaps for some females the higher amounts of time spent on computer use is a digital distraction. It is interesting that this time-use problem is not exhibited by males; that is, there was no relationship between large amounts of time spent on gaming and grades. The direction of influence in female digital distraction is not clear from our data. Whether there is a cycle that starts or ends with distraction needs to be examined more closely. Also, why males overall show no systematic digital distraction effect needs to be further examined. The dynamics of distraction clearly require more detailed study.

We need to keep the academic consequences of digital distraction for females in perspective. Overall, our female respondents do better at school than their male counterparts; 37% of females in Nunavut have at least an 80% average compared to 30% of Nunavut males, and the corresponding percentages in Nova Scotia are 62% and 44%. Females are not at an academic disadvantage.

Thus far, the digital divide has often been defined as "the separation of information haves from the have-nots" (Ono and Zavodny 2005, 106); however, this definition needs to be further developed. Often researchers assume that the digital divide will have consequences and that only through digital inclusion will these consequences disappear. For instance, Ilomaki and Rantanen (2007) argue that after digital inclusion was created, the students became "proficient enough to function constructively in the emerging knowledge society" (132). However our study has found that digital inclusion, for some females, is associated with negative academic consequences. Clearly inclusion is not the whole story and neither is skill. At some level the digital divide becomes the difference between those who know how to selectively control and contextualize computer technologies and those who are simply amazed, entertained, and consumed by technology as a distraction.

Notes

1 CHAID is CHi-squared Automatic Interaction Detection analysis. This technique identifies segments in a population that vary in relation to a dependent variable that is measured at the nominal or ordinal level. In this case we looked at types of computer use that vary with gender. Gaming and communication ended up being the top two computer usage types that differentiate on gender.

2 Latent Class Cluster analysis is a clustering technique that finds population segments based on categories of responses. In this case we are looking at population segments based on communicating and gaming indicators.
3 It is important to note that these models were run separately for each population. The relative differences are measured within each population.

WORKS CITED

Bannert, M. and P.R. Arbinger. 1996. "Gender-related Differences in Exposure to and Use of Computers: Results of a Survey of Secondary School Students." *European Journal of Psychology of Education* 11:269–82.

Bonanno, P. and P.A.M. Kommers 2005. "Gender Differences and Styles in the Use of Digital Games." *Educational Psychology* 25:13–41.

Ching, C.C., J.D. Basham, and E. Jang. 2005. "The Legacy of the Digital Divide: Gender, Socioeconomic Status, and Early Exposure as Predictors of Full-spectrum Technology Use among Young Adults." *Urban Education* 40:394–411.

Colley, A. and C. Comber. 2003. "Age and Gender Differences in Computer Use and Attitudes among Secondary School Students: What Has Changed?" *Educational Research* 45:155–65.

Colwell, J., C. Grady, and S. Rhaiti. 1995. "Computer Games, Self-esteem and Gratification Needs in Adolescents." *Journal of Community and Applied Social Psychology* 5:195–206.

Czerniewicz, L. and D. Ng'ambi. 2004. "Students' Use of Computers in UCT's 'Walk-in' Laboratories." *British Journal of Educational Technology* 35:241–46.

Durndell, A. 1991. "The Persistence of the Gender Gap in Computing." *Computers and Education* 16:283–87.

Durndell, A., P. Glissov, and G. Siann. 1995. "Gender and Computing: Persisting Differences." *Educational Research* 37:219–27.

Durndell, A. and K. Thomson 1997. "Gender and computing: A decade of change?" *Computers and Education* 28:1–9.

Durndell, A. and Z. Haag. 2002. "Computer Self Efficacy, Computer Anxiety, Attitudes toward the Internet and Reported Experience with the Internet, by Gender, in an East European Sample." *Computers in Human Behavior* 18:521–35.

Fife-Schaw, C., G.M. Breakwell, T. Lee, and J. Spencer. 1986. "Patterns of Teenage Computer Usage." *Journal of Computer Assisted Learning* 2:152–61.

Gross, E.F. 2004. "Adolescent Internet Use: What We Expect, What Teens Report." *Journal of Applied Developmental Psychology: An International Lifespan Journal* 25:633–49.

Harris, S. 1999. "Secondary School Students' Use of Computers at Home." *British Journal of Educational Technology* 30:331–40.

Harrison, A.W., R.K. Rainer Jr., and W.A. Hochwarter. 1997. "Gender Differences in Computing Activities." *Journal of Social Behavior and Personality* 12:849–68.

Herskovic, P., A. Vasquez, J. Herskovic, V. Herskovic, A. Roizen, M.T. Urrutia, et al. 2000. "Ownership of Computers and Abilities for Their Use in a Sample of Chilean Medical Students." *Medical Teacher* 22:197–99.

Houtz, L.E. and U.G. Gupta. 2001. "Nebraska High School Students' Computer Skills and Attitudes." *Journal of Research on Computing in Education* 33:316–27.

Ilomaki, L. and P. Rantanen. 2007. "Intensive Use of ICT in School: Developing Differences in Students' ICT Expertise." *Computers and Education* 48:119–36.

Jackson, L.A., K.S. Ervin, P.D. Gardner, and N. Schmitt. 2001. "Gender and the Internet: Women Communicating and Men Searching." *Sex Roles: A Journal of Research* 44:363–79.

Joiner, R., J. Gavin, J. Duffield, M. Brosnan, C. Crook, A. Durndell, et al. 2005. "Gender, Internet Identification, and Internet Anxiety: Correlates of Internet Use." *CyberPsychology and Behavior* 8:371–78.

Kafai, Y. B. and S. Sutton. 1999. "Elementary School Students' Computer and Internet Use at Home: Current Trends and Issues." *Journal of Educational Computing Research* 21:345–62.

Kent, N. and K. Facer. 2004. "Different Worlds? A Comparison of Young People's Home and School ICT Use." *Journal of Computer Assisted Learning* 20:440–55.

Kraut, Robert, Tridas Mukhopadhyay, Janusz Szczypula, Sara Kiesler, and Bill Scherlis. 1999. "Information and Communication: Alternative Uses of the Internet in Households." *Information Systems Research* 10:287–303.

Lee, A.C.K. 2003. "Undergraduate Students' Gender Differences in IT Skills and Attitudes." *Journal of Computer Assisted Learning* 19:488–500.

Lenhart, A., L. Rainie, and O. Lewis. 2001. "Teenage Life Online: The Rise of the Instant Message Generation and the Internet's Impact on Friendship and Family Relationships." Washington, DC: PEW Internet & American Life Project. http://www.pewinternet.org/Reports/2001/Teenage-Life-Online.aspx.

Leung, L. 2001. "College Student Motives for Chatting on ICQ." *New Media and Society* 3:483–501.

Li, K. and G. Kirkup. 2007. "Gender and Cultural Differences in Internet Use: A Study of China and the UK." *Computers and Education* 48:301–17.

Losh, S.C. 2004. "Gender, Educational, and Occupational Digital Gaps 1983–2002." *Social Science Computer Review* 22:152–66.

Messineo, M. and I.Y. DeOllos. 2005. "Are We Assuming Too Much? Exploring Students' Perception of Their Computer Competence." *College Teaching* 53:50–55.

Miller, L., H. Schweingruber, and C. Brandenburg. 2001. "Middle School Students' Technology Practices and Preferences: Re-examining Gender Differences." *Journal of Educational Multimedia and Hypermedia* 10:125–40.

Mumtaz, S. 2001. "Children's Enjoyment and Perception of Computer Use in the Home and the School." *Computers and Education* 36:347–62.

Odell, P., K. Korgen, P. Shumacher, and M. Delucchi. 2000. "Internet Use among Female and Male College Students." *CyberPsychology and Behavior* 3:855–62.

Ono, H. and M. Zavodny. 2005. "Gender Differences in Information Technology Usage: A U.S.–Japan Comparison." *Sociological Perspectives* 48:105–33.

Papastergiou, M. and C. Solomonidou. 2005. "Gender Issues in Internet Access and Favourite Internet Activities among Greek High School Pupils Inside and Outside School." *Computers and Education* 44:377–93.

Rajagopal, I. and N. Bojin. 2003. "'I Don't Do Windows': Gender, Pedagogy, and Instructional Technologies." *Education and Society* 21:75–97.

Singh, S. 2001. "Gender and the Use of the Internet at Home." *New Media and Society* 3:395–415.

Smith, B.N. and J.R. Necessary. 1996. "Assessing the Computer Literacy of Undergraduate College Students." *Education and Society* 117:188–93.

Stewart, K. and H.P. Choi. 2003. "PC-Bang (Room) Culture: A Study of Korean College Students' Private and Public Use of Computers and the Internet." *Trends in Communication* 11:36–80.

Subrahmanyam, K., P.M. Greenfield, R. Kraut, and E. Gross. 2001. "The Impact of Computer Use on Children's and Adolescents' Development." *Journal of Applied Developmental Psychology: An International Lifespan Journal* 22:385–401.

Thiessen, V. 2007. "Performance and Perception: Exploring Gender Gaps in Human Capital Skills." *Canadian Journal of Sociology* 32:145–76.

Van Dijk, J. and K. Hacker. 2003. "The Digital Divide as a Complex and Dynamic Phenomenon." *Information Society* 19:315–26.

Volman, M., E. van Eck, I. Heemskerk, and E. Kuiper. 2005. "New Technologies, New Differences: Gender and Ethnic Differences in Pupils' Use of ICT in Primary and Secondary Education." *Computers and Education* 45:35–55.

Weiser, E.B. 2000. "Gender Differences in Internet Use Patterns and Internet Application Preferences: A Two-sample Comparison." *CyberPsychology and Behavior* 3:167–78.

Young, B.J. 2000. "Gender Differences in Student Attitudes toward Computers." *Journal of Research on Computing in Education* 33:204–16.

Chapter 5

In the "ditch" or on the proverbial "information highway": An investigation of equity and technological literacies in the preparation and practice of teachers

Ted D. Naylor

Blye W. Frank

Canada has a long history of employing information communication technologies (ICTs) to advance and facilitate activities in the public sphere, or that civic "space" facilitating democratic citizenship, engagement, and participation (Dale & Naylor 2005). As a key institutional component of advanced social democracies or one constituent feature of what O'Connor (1973) terms the "legitimating function" of the state, the field of education has not surprisingly found itself taken up with a similar concern of how to incorporate technology to extend or enhance its capabilities. This chapter is generally concerned with how schools, teachers, students, and technology interact and how technologies potentially influence the educational system within the domain of teaching and bachelor-level post-secondary teaching education.

Although the question of how schools, teachers, students, and technology interact within the educational system appears to be a uniquely contemporary question, it is one that has long perplexed educators (Kerr 2005). Distinctive to the current social context, however, is the rapid pace and implementation of ICTs into today's classrooms and teacher training programs at the post-secondary level. This is particularly true in the context of how we now think about education and technology, and the crucial link between the two evidenced in emergent notions of ICT as a new and crucial form of literacy (Snyder 1998; Warschauer in press). With recent advances in ICTs, their diffusion, both real and imagined, throughout the social order has heightened the sense that we need to better understand how ICTs are being employed within pedagogical and educational settings. Indeed, an aggressive policy discourse surrounding education and training has emerged in advanced social democracies that explicitly links the role of education in creating human and social capital and in the production of new knowledge- and "education-related externalities" (OECD 2001).

There is a continued push, then, to incorporate ICTs in pedagogical and educational settings based on the contention that ICT can facilitate "students' communication, problem solving, decision making and expression" (Nova Scotia 2005, 6). As one of our interview participants, who teaches at a school of education observes, "We have a public school program that says one of our essential graduation learnings will be technical competence, and I don't believe we can have technological competence or literacy unless it's embedded in all the curriculums." This conceptualization and understanding of using technology in education is of course ontological in nature; it assumes technology as a particular kind of public good, embedding technology with a value manifest in better educational outcomes. This orientation to technology and education is captured by the tension to get on the proverbial "information highway" at the peril of students and learning remaining "in the ditch." At the most general level, it is the peril of those "stuck in the ditch" that forms the empirical and critical concern of the present discussion.

ICTs AND SOCIAL CAPITAL

As many of the chapters in this collection explore, there remain serious questions around the ability of ICT to deliver on its purported educational and social promises, particularly in terms of its capacity to contribute to or create social capital, considered necessary for developing skills for employment and mobility in today's complex world (Narayan 1999). This chapter therefore complements the preceding analyses by exploring the underlying processes through which technology and technological innovation become integrated and applied to contemporary education curriculum content. It does so by investigating the role of teachers (both student teachers and education faculty who teach student teachers) in taking up and implementing ICT in the classroom. In this way, it is primarily interested in the extent to which education faculty and student teachers are prepared to use ICT in the classroom. In short, we are after their routine and everyday expectations and experiences of, with, and about technology, from both the perspective of those teaching in the Bachelor of Education programs and those being taught.

Similar to the other chapters in this collection, our analysis tackles these questions through the lens of social capital and equity. Equity problematizes the everyday organization of teaching/teachers and technology by taking seriously that the ruling relations of education can be exclusive or hegemonic (Smith 1987), marginalizing historically disadvantaged groups. Additionally, it asks us to consider that in any given setting, technology can deepen inequity and stultify opportunity just as easily as enlighten and/or educate (Blacker & McKie 2002). Social capital highlights the tangible features of one's social network, or that "aggregate of the actual or potential resources which are linked to possession of a durable network of more or less institutionalized relationships of mutual acquaintance and recognition" (Bourdieu 1986, 248). The notions of "bonding" and "bridging" social capital in relation to ICTs, moreover, ask us to evaluate the kinds of activities and resources that may or may not be factors in supporting and creating advantageous social networks and improving individuals' circumstances through ICTs within education, particularly for individuals or communities identified as socially disadvantaged or excluded. As Gewirtz et al. (2005) note, research in the area of social capital typically posits a causal relationship between the degree of social bonds within families and communities on one hand and children's achievement at school and their potential future economic prosperity on the other. Given the purported linkages between social capital and inclusive educational attainment,[1] coupled with the introduction of ICT to instructional practice to enhance learning, information diffusion, networking, and skill capacity, careful attention to equity around ICTs is paramount to ensure that the potential benefits of ICTs are inclusive and beneficial to all learners.

Previous chapters have, in different ways, focused on an empirical evaluation of ICT around equity to achieve or build forms of social capital in terms of both bridging and bonding social capital. Our chapter evaluates the possibility of social capital at a broader organizational/pedagogical level, investigating teachers' and student teachers' capacity and understanding of why they will incorporate technology into the educational enterprise and to what end. If ICT literacy is now commonly understood as key to creating the potential for crucial forms of social capital,[2] evidenced by an impressive mix of infrastructure, resources, and policy efforts aimed at increasing ICT literacy within the past decade, then we must pay careful attention to those educational processes that may or may not confine certain populations to the ditch of the information highway.

METHODOLOGY

This chapter explores equity issues in teaching and learning technology and presents data from faculty and student–teacher interviews, focus groups, and surveys in faculties of Education in Nova Scotia, Canada. Twenty-six semi-structured interviews and six focus groups with faculty and students in were carried out as a means of examining whether teachers are being prepared to be "technologically literate." We are interested in how they understand issues of technology and teaching as it relates to their educational careers.

Thirteen interviews were conducted with faculty from the three faculties of education in Atlantic Canada. Ten interviews were conducted with second-year Bachelor of Education students, and three interviews were conducted with members from the education community in Nova Scotia to provide additional context and insight into the issues under exploration. Second-year students were explicitly targeted because, in accordance with the degree requirements of the department, each student would have had the opportunity to complete an in-class practicum teaching in a classroom setting and would be able to provide insights and experiences that first-year students could not. Additionally, six separate focus groups with second-year Bachelor of Education students were conducted at two faculties of education. The interviews attempt to elicit data around equity and technology by asking respondents for their views on whether and if current teaching practices are, in fact, equitable.[3]

Although an obvious limitation of the study is that it did not explicitly canvass a broad, representative sample of current teachers in the system, the focus on faculties of education and student teachers provides us with an opportunity to investigate a research sample that is actively engaged in discussions and learning around technology, coloured implicitly by debates around technology as a value in terms of its effectiveness and usefulness for teaching. If teachers' prior knowledge mediates future learning (Borko & Putnam 1996), and if in learning situations teachers interpret, question, or evaluate new knowledge through their previously acquired knowledge and experiences (Bransford & Schwartz 1999), then how faculties of education and their students currently understand and incorporate technology into the educational enterprise becomes an essential path of empirical enquiry. This analysis is relevant to how student teachers will or will not incorporate technology into their future teaching practices because it provides us insights into their current understandings and experiences. It also provides insights into the capacity of future teachers to engage issues of equity around technology-infused classroom experiences that are currently being put forward by departments of education and curriculum reform in Canada as a core pedagogical skill and goal.

Finally, a comprehensive survey was administered to students in the above-mentioned education programs. The survey questions posed closed-ended questions around issues of equity and technology, framed by the students' experiences as teachers-in-training, and asked them to provide some basic demographic information about themselves. The survey was completed by 141 second-year Bachelor of Education students. The quantitative data were organized using basic descriptive frequencies. An examination of the curriculum in three different Bachelor of Education programs was incorporated into the data analysis.

ICT CURRICULUM REFORM, EQUITY, AND SOCIAL CAPITAL

The value of education has increased dramatically due to changes in the socio-economic structure of Canada (Canadian Council on Learning 2005). Beginning in the 1980s, a global policy discourse surrounding education and training has emerged across the advanced industrial world (Lloyd & Payne 2003). A central thrust behind this discourse is the notion of "knowledge economies" emerging in tight competition with one another, played out through the now-global pressures of the market, where states must compete on economic terms, exploiting the commercial advantages offered by a more autonomous, well-educated, and flexible workforce (Lloyd & Payne 2003). In this vein, "new growth theory" has been very influential in highlighting the role of education in creating social and human capital (OECD 2001) and in the production of new knowledge- and education-related externalities. Intensifying global competition, coupled with the rapid proliferation and acceleration of advanced ICTs, is understood to have formed the basis of a new global order and competitive environment, as well as new demands on educational policy and practice (Angus 2004). As a result, the promotion of educational reform has increasingly become a central component of labour-market strategies in Canada, underpinned by the "need for education and training that are relevant to globally competitive economic development" (Wotherspoon 1998, 130).

Not surprisingly, then, the education literature clearly argues that high school completion, for example, benefits the individual and society as a whole (Canadian Council on Learning 2005). At the same time, empirical evidence reveals that, conversely, the socio-economic consequences for students who drop out of the education system remain bleak. Data from the Statistics Canada Labour Force Survey (LFS), for example, demonstrate that only about 62% of high school drop-outs between ages of 20–24 were employed in 2004–05 (Canadian Council on Learning 2005). The importance of a basic high school education in connection to higher degrees of labour force participation, employability, and income has been clearly demonstrated by research in this area (Thiessen 2001). In this context, and as ICT is now being positioned as an essential feature and skill competency of the educational career for youth, the role of teacher knowledge and experience in forming ICT-integrated pedagogy is increasingly important (Hughes 2005).

Historically, well-documented research pertaining to the area of education and literacy suggests that marginalized groups in Canada, particularly African Canadian and Mi'kmaq youth in Atlantic Canada, have low levels of literacy (Lax 2001; Schon, Sanyal, and Mitchell 2001). As a result, people marginalized due to differences in culture, gender, and socioeconomic status experience limitations in employability and educational opportunities. In a Canadian schooling context, however, the apparent requirements of a knowledge economy provide yet a new impetus and increased emphasis on increasing the current knowledge and skills of students, requiring the improved achievement of all students. As the Department of Education in Nova Scotia states, the context of students' ICT use is that "lifelong learning and employment in the information economy demand fluency and critical engagement with new media texts.... Through the influence of ICT, Nova Scotian learners have the opportunity to access, use, and augment human knowledge more quickly and comprehensively than ever before" (Nova Scotia 2005, 5, 7). According to Milton (2003, 2), this need to improve student achievement can be described as raising the bar and closing the gap: "that is raising the overall average performance of Canadian students in international comparisons and narrowing (or eliminating) the difference between the achievement of students from lower socio-economic contexts and those from more affluent backgrounds."

In this sense, ICT literacy is presented as a desirable and necessary form of inclusive social and human capital, particularly in relation to marginalized students and, for educators, in relation to the increasing emphasis on educational success within the context of a knowledge economy. One of the key assumptions within education curriculum reform around the introduction of ICTs, then, is that the large-scale introduction of ICT into learning environments will improve learning outcomes for *all* students (Milton 2003), effectively getting them onto the information highway with all of the advantages presumed by this now ubiquitous metaphor. Bransford et al. (1999, cited in Volman & van Eck 2001), for example, categorize ICT applications within education by how they can help improve education and learning, which includes improved problem solving for "real-life" problems, improved problem solving through collaborative or cooperative learning, and new learning processes facilitated by connections between the school and the outside world. It is through these kinds of bonding and bridging social-capital-building capacities that ICTs are thought to hold potential for better teaching and learning outcomes.

Although the introduction of ICTs into educational curriculum at the teacher, student, education, and provincial-policy level in Canada (see Nova Scotia 2005) continues to operate with the conviction that "information technology is one of the engines needed to drive the necessary transformation of the education system" (Royal Commission on Learning 1994, cited in Wotherspoon 1998: 207), this conviction becomes more problematic when we consider it in relation to equity. If we are to consider competence with technology as the "new" literacy (Snyder 1998) and we understand that members of marginalized communities, particularly youth, are already disadvantaged, the implications of a deepening digital divide for this population are especially relevant; further disparities, divisions, and gaps in ICT may be perpetuated, sustaining low levels of literacy. If people are not provided with the means to access the information highway, their potential to build knowledge and skill capacity around ICT will be impeded. Being left in the ditch not only exacerbates existing disparities but also creates new barriers, thereby contributing to an expanding and deepening digital divide.

Scholars of the digital divide now point out that this divide cannot be reduced to just technological access, solved through "simple technological fixes" (Parayil 2005). To this end, the analytical concept of social capital helps to draw our attention past technological fixes by asking us to consider ICT literacy in relation to the actual or potential resources that individuals can mobilize through their individual and social networks, as well as the importance of such mobilization to an individual's success. Of course, and as Bourdieu (1986) argues, social capital is complex and is generated and used differently in various contexts, often in ways that can act as a basis for reproducing inequality. In short, social capital problematizes ICTs in connection to equity because it critically highlights what is at stake for those who might be stuck in the ditch on the information highway. How can we ensure that the benefits of ICTs within education do not confine traditionally marginalized populations to the proverbial ditch? If "information and communication technology should be integrated within inclusive classrooms" where "all learners have equitable opportunities to reach their potential" (Nova Scotia 2005, 6), how do we ensure this happens?

Researchers in the areas of education and technology identify teachers as being the link, or the "linchpin," to helping people, especially youth, build ICT knowledge and skill capacity (Weinman & Haag 1999, 48). The power to develop innovative technology-supported pedagogy rests with the teacher's interpretation of the value of ICTs in the classroom (Hughes 2005). This interpretation is mediated by past experience and accumulated knowledge (Bransford & Schwartz 1999); therefore, the training of teachers at the post-secondary level is a crucial factor in any successful implementation of ICT in the classroom setting. Young, Hall, and Clarke (2007, 92) note that while competing notions of teachers' work and the nature of the teaching profession differ across different professional teacher-education programs, teacher preparation can be characterized as essentially a *generative* practice, a *replicative* practice of socialization and induction, and a *prescriptive* practice to prepare new teachers to implement a larger government agenda. Teachers who are therefore knowledgeable in effective and equitable pedagogical methods, who are comfortable with and proficient in technological applications and tools, will be able to appropriately integrate technology into their classrooms, providing opportunities for better learning outcomes (Volman & van Eck 2001). As Hughes (2005, 279) observes, "Teachers who learn about technology may connect it to their subject matter knowledge, pedagogical knowledge, and pedagogical content knowledge." Research suggests further that teachers' attitudes and beliefs toward technology are of great importance in their decisions to adopt and frequently use ICT in the classroom (Russell et al. 2003, 307), and that positive computer attitudes can be developed through interaction between student teachers and mentor teachers who promote the appropriate context of computer use in the classroom (Kadijevich 2006, 441).

Teachers can therefore play an essential role in the realization of a more inclusive education if they are provided with opportunities to acquire familiarity with ICTs. In recognition of the role teachers can play, we now turn our attention to investigating whether current teaching practices are delivering the essential skills and understanding required to build our students' technological capacity, an important aspect of both social capital and equity. As the push to incorporate ICTs into education continues unabated (Milton 2003), it is necessary to investigate and explore the extent to which university faculty in teacher-education programs are becoming proficient at using ICT, both in terms of their ability to use technology for their own instruction and, by extension, that of their students.

FINDINGS
ICT access
Technological inequities are most visible in terms of access to and integration of resources. Studies on teaching and learning have consistently demonstrated differences in participation, skill level, and attitudes toward ICT according to gender, geographic location, age, and culture, as well as socioeconomic status of schools, communities, and individuals (see, for example, Looker and Thiessen 2003; Weinman and Haag 1999). Typically, the literature has conceptualized this inequity around access as a "digital divide" based on an unequal distribution or diffusion of new technologies. The social capital benefits associated with ICTs potentially embedded in the access and use of computers, software, and Internet connections are expensive; when this equipment is not available to everyone in a community, learning or otherwise, historical social inequalities can be reproduced (Wotherspoon 1998, 210). In traditional terms of access, the findings of this study suggest that there two key digital divides still operating within the faculties of education in Nova Scotia, as well as a perceived digital divide in the classrooms of the provincial education system.

The faculties of education data clearly reveal that there are a number of limitations with respect to effectively integrating technology into the curriculum in university classrooms, accordingly influencing the preparation and capacity of new teachers to become ICT literate. "Money equals technological literacy ... whether it's money at home, or money put into the actual school without money you don't have technology ... [without technology] no technological literacy" (faculty interview participant). As our interview participant notes, the notion of a digital divide based on access continues to be understood as an important obstacle to building ICT literacy and hence equitable social capital. Although some scholars caution against seeing the digital divide as the absence of a technical artifact and lack of connectivity, suggesting this is too instrumental and reductive (Parayil 2005), access to technology nevertheless remains a core issue to ICT literacy. Regardless of academic theory or critique, or the perception that this is an "old" issue seemingly resolved, the physical presence of a computer, equipment, hardware, and Internet connection remains a persistent and fundamental obstacle to ICT literacy. Asked if they (i.e., teaching faculty) are being encouraged to incorporate technology into their teaching, one interview participant comments that, "it has been encouraged since I've been here but like I said before, the faculty will say well, that's very nice, but we need equipment, if we're going to talk about technology, we can't just talk about it, we need the equipment" (faculty interview participant). Another faculty member notes in relation to her efforts to incorporate technology in the classroom: "I use a laptop, I try to access the Internet, but at this point it depends on what room I'm in [in] the building" (faculty interview participant). Another faculty member, who also teaches in the secondary school system, observes that when attempting to incorporate innovative software to her teaching curriculum, "at this point I've had to either borrow them from school boards, or share my materials, my own stuff, and lend it out to them [the students]" (faculty interview participant). The general observation that "a lot of professors are really frustrated with the antiquated technology" (faculty interview participant) speaks to a basic, yet persistent, obstacle to overcoming a digital divide based on access in the faculties of education interviewed in this study.

   Secondly, our interview participants noted a similarly long-identified, well-understood yet still persistent digital divide based on traditional access to ICTs within Nova Scotia schools. The student teachers reported dramatic disparities in access during their in-class teaching practicums, with significant differences in the availability and accessibility of technology in schools and classrooms throughout the province of Nova Scotia: "When I did my practicum ... that was a school that had all the computers.... Now ... see when I went to [different school name], they didn't have computers in the classroom or at home" (student teacher interview participant). And: "You go into a classroom like last year for my practicum ... in a brand-new school where every class has six computers, and there's computer labs all over the place—that's awesome! But, then I go to a school this year, where there might be two working computers ... for six different classes" (student teacher interview participant).

Typical of many comments reported from our interview participants, these sorts of comments speak directly to both real and perceived disparities around basic access to ICTs found within and among schools and educational settings. There is a general feeling that access to and, correspondingly, literacy with ICTs in schools depends very much upon the school in question and how the staff at that particular school may or may not incorporate technology into pedagogy and curriculum: "I'm finding that the students say that there is a big difference in the schools, in the secondary schools. We had one student come in, and she said there's no availability of computers, there was one lab ... it was very difficult to book. So she said she was very disappointed that she wasn't able to use a lot of her skills" (faculty interview participant).

In a discussion of access and availability of equipment at schools, both faculty members and student teachers were at a loss to explain how and why schools had disparate levels of technology present. Typical comments from our sample included "I've heard that mostly the reason why there might not be equipment at a particular school is because the principal is not technologically literate" (faculty interview participant), "I don't know why people get new schools [with technology]" (faculty interview participant), and "We do find with all the high schools, that their literacy with technology goes up and down depending on the faculty" (faculty interview participant).

An empirical survey of the ratio of students to all computers across the eight school boards in our sample indicates that the kind of comments expressed by faculty and student teachers around access are not without merit. Figure 5.1 shows a wide numerical discrepancy of computers across the eight school boards and across different grades. It should come as no surprise, then, that participants in our study report both frustration and bewilderment about access to ICTs throughout schools in the province. Figure 5.2 also makes visible these claims of inequitable access by demonstrating the percentage of classrooms with three or more computers across the different school types in the province.

Both the recently built "P3" schools (those built through a public–private partnership agreement with the province),[4] and those even more recently constructed demonstrate that these schools are significantly advantaged in terms of access to computers at school. In a survey of second-year student teachers, 90% indicated that more access to computers was needed for their

FIGURE 5.1

Ratio of students to all computers in Nova Scotia across school boards

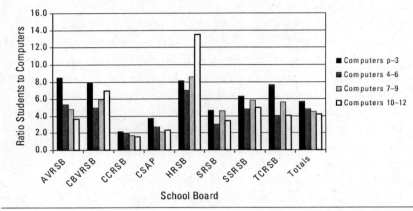

Source: Nova Scotia 2006.

FIGURE 5.2

Classrooms with three or more "current" computers in Nova Scotia

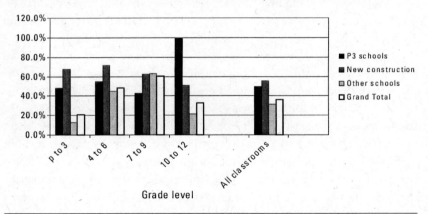

Source: Nova Scotia 2006.

students in order for them to use ICTs more effectively in the classroom based on their practicum experience. Similarly, 91% of survey respondents indicated that more access is also "probably" or "definitely" needed to software that is curricular-based (data not shown).

The data from this study suggest that the traditional notion of a digital divide still exists as a persistent and identifiable feature of education in Nova Scotia. Whether informed by the figures above or not, faculty at the schools of education, along with their students, explicitly recognize that the access to ICTs in schools are far from systemically uniform, that there are "high-tech" schools and others with considerably less technology. Understood in this way, providing literacy with ICTs for students is obviously problematized in terms of access to technology in post-secondary education programs. Reaping the benefits of ICT literacy encompassed in concepts such as social capital becomes seriously compromised if neither student teachers nor the schools themselves are equipped to adequately create these skills. As Looker and Thiessen (2003) surmise, the presence of a digital divide ultimately compromises the goal of equity and access to ICT and ICT-related skills. Moreover, the experiences of student teachers during their practicums underlines the difficulties of trying to teach within an ICT-integrated pedagogical approach given the disparities in access to ICTs within the current education system. This becomes doubly complicated when the faculties of education report their own difficulties in overcoming issues of access around ICT literacy within both teaching and curriculum. Although the discourse around the digital divide continues to broaden and emphasize the importance of how ICTs are used (Warschauer 2002), coupled with attending to the social, political, and economic context around ICT and access (Sassen 2005), our study suggests that basic access remains as a persistent feature of a digital divide in the province of Nova Scotia, both at the level of teacher education and at least potentially within the education system itself.

ICT integration

It was a common theme among students in the Bachelor of Education programs that integrating technology into curriculum is minimal or nonexistent. Seventy-seven percent of student teachers reported that more resources are needed to better illustrate how to integrate technology into the curriculum, and over half of students interviewed (55%) indicated that they "definitely/probably" needed more training with technology. These findings are supported by other studies that have found that teacher-training programs do not provide future teachers "with the kinds of experiences necessary to prepare them to use technology effectively in their classrooms" (Milken Exchange on Education Technology 1999, i). The students also reported that there was a lack of teacher training with ICT and a critical lack of ICT courses in Bachelor of Education programs. Many reported an impression that faculty did not know how to use software or equipment. Comments such as "I don't feel as if we're walking away with tools for once we get into the classroom, about what do we do (in the classroom with technology)!" (student teacher participant), "I think they've (name of school) spent too much time talking about the larger issues with technology ... but when it gets down to the ... to the thumbtacks, we're on our own!" (student teacher participant) and "Well ... anything that I learned here in the B.Ed. [Bachelor of Education] program [with technology], I feel that I already knew before" (student teacher participant) were common among the focus groups and interviews with student teachers. The data suggest that overall there is a critical lack of ICT integration within the faculties of education.

Notably, data from the faculty corroborates the student teacher claims. Faculty generally perceive their own ICT literacy as poor and neither well supported nor well developed: "so, our classrooms are presently being equipped with multimedia equipment, but even with that equipment, it doesn't mean that necessarily people know what to do with it, and I find that my faculty's talk around technology is around PowerPoint ... it's basically around presentation and not any other use" (faculty interview participant). And: "Nobody teaches it (technology). Like I don't have an English teacher walking a around with a sense of urgency to promote (the) technological competency goal. I don't think any teacher outside of a computer lab has one iota of concern whether or not a student reaches that eagle ... the first thing they would say is the kids know more than we do" (faculty member participant).

This finding is similar to what other studies of teacher-training programs have demonstrated with respect to technology: few hours of actual technology training and, often, training focused on the mechanics of technology rather than effective teaching strategies. If we consider that the ability to operate various components of hardware and software does not constitute an "acceptable level of proficiency for faculty in teacher education programs" (Otero et al. 2005, 9), then the data reported here around ICT integration become even more troubling.

Comments from participants in this study suggest further that there is a critical lack of ICT in courses and the overall curriculum of the Bachelor of Education programs: "Presently, we have one course ... it's a required course for secondary only ... we do offer a media and technology and communication course, an option or an elective for elementary students, but it is an elective, and so only a few, you know a dozen maybe out of sixty students take that course ... that goes beyond, you know, the power point presentation" (faculty interview participant). Also: "In fact, there has not been discussion around what students need to know when they go out into the schools [regarding integrating technology into classrooms]" (faculty interview participant).

Notably, both faculty and student teachers reported minimal use of technology for more advanced tasks, and related that when they used technology, either in their own studies or their practicums, it typically meant using computers and programs for simple, "lower-cognitive" tasks, such as typing drills or basic word processing rather than innovative strategies that engaged students in active, constructive, "higher-cognitive" learning opportunities (Volman & van Eck 2001). Survey results in this study generally reported that students felt their Bachelor of Education programs did not greatly improve or expand their skills in technology. Asked if they need more opportunities to work with colleagues using technology-enhanced curriculum units, 77% responded "probably/definitely," with only 5% responding "definitely/probably not." Other studies report similar findings, noting that the pedagogical use of technology is typically left to the individual instructor in teacher-education programs. They are left to not only develop the base skills by themselves, but to "construct an understanding of the pedagogical use of technology" in their classroom (Otero et al. 2005, 10). The data in our sample certainly confirm that capacities and integration of ICT with respect to faculty and student teachers largely remains at an instrumental or task-orientated level, and that a deeper, integrated pedagogical orientation to ICTs as an educational tool is rarely available in the faculties of education that make up our sample. Milton's (2003, 2) observation, that "in the absence of statements of explicit objectives and desired outcomes, it is difficult to define what success in ICT integration looks like," succinctly characterizes the integration of ICT (or lack thereof) into both pedagogy and curriculum within the faculties of education of this study.

ICT literacy

The simplest way to conceptualize ICT access is as access to a computer device or set of devices. Warschauer (in press) observes that, although access to a computing device is clearly an essential first step (and the data from our sample strongly suggests that it remains an issue for faculties of education and student teachers, as well as for the education system in the province), access itself does not necessarily guarantee any degree of ICT literacy. As one interview participant succinctly reminds us, "twenty computers in a school doesn't make it a computer literate school" (student interview participant).

Although this comment seems to reflect common sense, it brings us to what might be described as a second-generation literature around the digital divide, which conceptualizes access as a set of meaningful social practices (Warschauer in press). Older ICTs such as television and radio have reached wide saturation points across the traditional divides based on socio-economic status, age, gender, and ethnicity, for example. The use of advanced ICTs is likely to follow a similar pattern in Canada over the coming decade. Statistics Canada reports that use of ICTs in Canada continues to grow. For example, two-thirds of adult Canadians used the Internet in 2005, and an estimated 7.9 million Canadian households (61%) were connected to the Internet that same year (Statistics Canada 2006). In the case of ICTs, however, in order to broaden and deepen our understanding of access we must recognize that "other issues such as differential access to human and social capital will continue to play a role in fostering digital inequality" (Warschauer in press, 3). Whereas the digital divide around access to a computer or technological device centres on the presence of that device, access centred on ICT *literacy* highlights the social basis of literacy learning as a set of practices that varies in different social contexts across groups and individuals equipped with different levels of social capital. As Warschauer (in press, 14) argues, "by better understanding ICT access, we can also better promote it and thus help overcome social exclusion."

Ironically, it is believed by many observers that students today, including students in Bachelor of Education programs, are already armed with an advantageous and emerging social capital that is technologically literate. This is important, since "in consideration of the two-way relationship between social capital and ICTs, the predominant view is that high levels of social capital have a positive influence on ICT appropriation" (European Commission 2004, 11). In this respect, and within the field of education, there is a now commonly held view that students are generally familiar and "savvy" with technology in ways that are new and that present new challenges for the education system. As Farmer (2003) contends, "students are more technology literate and Internet-savvy than ever, and they use technology in ways that weren't even imagined a decade ago. Their fluency in technology is not even in question." One interview participant asks: "Where else in the history of civilization can ten-year-olds perform more complicated tasks using technologies than adults?" (faculty member participant). Some observers conclude that as new teachers who have grown-up with computers enter the teaching profession, their competencies with ICTs will lead to an increased use of technology for instruction (U.S Department of Education, cited in Russell et al. 2003). Considering that the evidence suggests that ICTs are empowering for bridging and bonding social capital (European Commission 2004), a high degree of ICT literacy present within teacher-education programs would seem to bode well for social capital and educational attainment, coupled with the associated socio-economic benefits attributed to high degrees of social capital.

Upon closer inspection, however, and considering the data in our study, the notion that today's students, both at the post-secondary level and throughout the secondary system, are technology literate is more problematic. Although students generally ranked their own computer ability as moderately high (a mean of 5 on a linear scale of 1–7, 1 being "no ability" and 7 being "expert ability"), they notably ranked the students in their practicum almost as high (4), suggesting little overall difference in literacy around ICTs between students and student teachers. Given the significant response of the student teachers in the survey who reported the need for better training (55%) and more opportunities (76%) to learn how to use technology-enhanced curriculums in the teacher-education programs, we cautiously challenge the assumption that student teachers possess high degrees of technological literacy with ICTs. Indeed, several interview participants within the ranks of faculty noted that the technological competence of incoming students was poor to dismal: "When I first started teaching this course, I came into it thinking I'm going to be teaching a group of students who, most them were born in 1982, so they've always known computers. So my assumption was that every one of these students would have a general level of technological competence that would allow me to have a starting point, and oh my god—they did not!" (faculty interview participant). And: "In fact, when I query my students in the department, I always ask them at the beginning of the course, how many of you are comfortable using computers. And I get maybe three out of thirty … it's a surprise, like, how did you get through your undergraduate career? And so I find their literacy level very low" (faculty interview participant).

Although student teachers in our sample remain optimistic around using ICTs within the classroom, with 75% of respondents indicating that its impact is positive or very positive and 78% agreeing that they like teaching courses with computers, the data from within the teacher training programs suggest that assumptions around students as technically literate may not be accurate. As the data suggest, the lack of literacy with ICT with respect to student teachers appears to be exacerbated by a lack of ICT integration into the curriculum of the education programs, as well as a reported lack of literacy of the faculty. These findings are tangentially supported by other studies that have found that teachers lack an understanding of how technology can be integrated and used for legitimate pedagogical purposes (Otero et al. 2005; Russell et al. 2003), suggesting a critical lack of ICT literacy among school teachers generally. These findings raise important questions around the ability of education programs to effectively prepare teachers for classrooms and educational settings that are increasingly premised on using ICT to teach and learn. When we consider that students also reported that issues of equity and technology access were often not addressed in their Bachelor of Education course work (a mean of 3.3 along a linear scale of 1–never discussed to 7–frequently discussed), along with reporting a need for "more access" (90%), then the implications of a deepening digital divide for traditionally marginalized populations becomes especially relevant given the current emphasis on ICT-integrated pedagogy and curriculum within the education system.

CONCLUSIONS

The data presented here around ICT literacy highlights the need to better articulate and incorporate ICT literacy into the professional programs at the post-secondary level. As Hughes (2005, 279) notes, knowledge is essential because teachers use it to determine actions in the classroom; "Thus it is strategic to identify the relevant knowledge base teachers draw on and develop when learning to teach with technology." Our data suggest that faculties of education have done a poor job of identifying a common or core base of ICT competency for both themselves and, by extension, their students. Although there is an assumption of high ICT literacy for student teachers entering education programs, it is not taught systematically at either the high school level or within the faculty programs themselves. We add, in that case, that it is also strategic to recognize that if today's students are increasingly required to incorporate and demonstrate high levels of ICT literacy to ensure their success into the future, then tomorrow's teachers better be clear and comfortable about what literacy with ICT is. In this way, they will be in a better position to ensure that literacy is taught for the betterment of all students. In addition, although the results clearly convey that student teachers are comfortable with potentially using technology, they more critically identify a significant lack of training for these students within their programs of study. Again, considering the continued push at the secondary levels of education across Canada to employ ICT-integrated pedagogy, the gap between teacher education and practice becomes particularly problematic for groups historically marginalized by the education system. The uneven distribution of computers across schools in Nova Scotia, for example, also highlights the need to ensure equitable access to ICTs within a school system. There is clearly a critical need to increase collaboration between faculties of education and Nova Scotia Department of Education. Positive and established partnerships and linkages will allow for information flow, particularly on issues pertaining to resources and improvements to technological updates and upgrades in software and equipment. At the same time, the development of a standard level of technology integrated into the Bachelor of Education course curriculum would ensure teachers learn and implement effective routine strategies to incorporate technology into the classroom. These courses must reach beyond that of a basic computer course if the assumptions around ICTs and benefits to curriculum and pedagogy are to be realized.

The data therefore bring us back to a critical re-examination of the digital divide based on equitable access with respect to ICT literacy. Simply because students today *appear* to be exposed to new technologies does not necessarily denote literacy with ICTs; nor should we assume a common experience among faculty or student teachers or students with technology. As studies have shown, learning is as much about enculturation as about transmission or discovery (Warschauer in press). Human learning takes place within communities of practice, embedded with varying degrees of human and social capital that can reproduce inequities around access. When we consider the empirical evidence of a still-persistent digital divide based on traditional inequities, particularly among historically marginalized populations, we need to be careful about the latent assumptions around ICT literacy and education. Robertson (2003) notes that the problems associated with the current rush to incorporate ICTs into education amount to a "presence of absence," that is, the absence of a critical and informed debate about what the meaning and worth of ICTs are in connection to education. Critical pedagogy and feminist analysis has clearly demonstrated that "silencing" occurs when some forms of knowledge, behavior, or competencies are privileged while others remain marginalized (Wotherspoon 1998). The data presented here suggest that not only does a traditional digital divide based on access problematize equity and social capital around ICTs, but that overall there is a lack of literacy with ICTs at the Faculty of Education level. As ICT literacy continues to be pushed as a crucial form of capital for students, then we must attend to the peril of those students and experiences who remain at risk of being silenced by technology—those "stuck in the ditch" on the information highway. The data from the faculties of education in this study support the position that until the silence around equity and ICTs becomes deafening, the teachers of tomorrow will continue to struggle and be poorly armed to effectively integrate ICTs into a truly equitable pedagogy and curriculum.

NOTES

1 It's worth noting that there considerable debate around the meaning of social capital and the empirical foundations of claims between social capital and educational attainment (Gewirtz et al. 2005). That said, this study is investigating the actual and current implementation and use of ICTs within the education system, which is based on notions of ICTs as beneficial to education and therefore to students' achievement and success.
2 The World Bank now compiles a range of statistics in recognition of the social and economic benefits of social capital (see http://www1.worldbank.org/prem/poverty/scapital/topic/info1.htm).
3 As indicated in the Introduction to this collection, there are no equivalent teacher education programs for secondary school teachers in Nunavut, hence our focus on programs in Nova Scotia.
4 In 1999, the Liberal provincial government came to power having pledged to build fifty-five P3 schools. The program was cut in 2003 with the election of a new Conservative government.

WORKS CITED

Angus, L. 2004. "Globalization and Educational Change: Bringing about the Reshaping and Re-norming of Practice." *Journal of Education Policy* 19:23–41.

Blacker, D. and J. McKie. 2002. "Information and Communication Technology: Educational Technology as Revealing and Concealing." In *The Blackwell Guide to the Philosophy of Education*, ed. N. Blake, P. Smeyer, R. Smith, and P. Standish, 234–52. Malden, MA: Blackwell.

Borko, H. and R.T. Putnam. 1996. "Teachers: Beliefs and Knowledge." In *Handbook of Educational Psychology*, ed. D. C. Berliner and R.C. Calfee, 709–25. New York: Macmillan.

Bourdieu, P. 1986. "The Forms of Capital." In *Handbook of Theory and Research for the Sociology of Education*, ed. J. Richardson, 241–58. London: Greenwood Press.

Bransford, J.D. and D.L. Schwartz. 1999. "Rethinking Transfer: A Simple Proposal with Multiple Implications." In *Review of Research in Education*, ed. G. P. Baxter, A. Iran-Nejad, and P.D. Pearson, 61–100. Washington, DC: American Educational Research Association.

Canadian Council on Learning. 2005. "Good News: Canada's High School Dropout Rates Are Falling." *Lessons in Learning.* http://www.ccl-cca.ca/CCL/Reports/ LessonsInLearning/LiL-16Dec2005.htm.

Dale, A. and D.T. Naylor. 2005. "Dialogue and Public Space: An Exploration of Radio and Information Communications Technologies." *Canadian Journal of Political Science/Revue canadienne de science politique* 38:203–25.

European Commission. 2004. "ICTs and Social Capital in the Knowledge Economy: Report on a Joint DG JRC/DG Employment Workshop."

Farmer, R. 2003. "Instant Messaging—Collaborative Tool or Educator's Nightmare!" Conference Proceedings, NAweb Conference, Web-based Learning Conference, University of New Brunswick. http://www.unb.ca/naweb/proceedings/ 2003/PaperFarmer.html.

Gewirtz, S., M. Dickson, S. Power, D. Halpin, and G. Whitty. 2005. "The Deployment of Social Capital Theory in Educational Policy and Provision: The Case of Action Zones in England." *British Educational Research Journal* 32:651–73.

Hughes, J. 2005. "The Role of Teacher Knowledge and Learning Experiences in Forming Technology-Integrated Pedagogy." *Journal of Technology and Teacher Education* 13:277–302.

Kadijevich, D. 2006. "Achieving Educational Technology Standards: The Relationship between Student Teacher's Interest and Institutional Support Offered." *Journal of Computer Assisted Learning* 22:437–43.

Kerr, S.T. 2005. "Why We All Want It to Work: Towards a Culturally Based Model for Technology and Educational Change." *British Journal of Educational Technology* 36:1005–16.

Lax, S. 2001. *Access Denied in the Information Age.* New York: Palgrave.

Lloyd, C. and J. Payne. 2003. "The Political Economy of Skill and the Limits of Educational Policy." *Journal of Education Policy* 18:85–107.

Looker, E.D. and V. Thiessen. 2003. "Beyond the Digital Divide in Canadian Schools: From Access to Competency in the Use of Information Technology." *Social Science Computer Review* 21:475–90.

Milken Exchange on Technology. 1999. *Will New Teachers Be Prepared to Teach in a Digital Age? A National Survey on Information Technology in Teacher Education.* http://www.mff.org/publications/publications.taf?page=154.

Milton, P. 2003. "Trends in the Integration of ICT and Learning in K–12 Systems." Canadian Education Association. http://www.cea-ace.ca/media/en/Trends _ICT_Integration.pdf.

Narayan, D. 1999. "Bonds and Bridges: Social Capital and Poverty." Policy Research Working Paper, No. 2167. World Bank. http://www.psigeorgia.org/pregp/ files/social%20capital.pdf.

Nova Scotia. 2005. "Information and Communication Technology in Public Schools." Learning Resources and Technology, Nova Scotia Department of Education.

———. 2006. "Survey of Classroom Computers in Nova Scotia Schools." Nova Scotia Department of Education.

O'Connor, J. 1973. *The Fiscal Crisis of the State.* New York: St. Martin's Press.

Organization for Economic Co-operation and Development. 1996. "The Knowledge-based Economy." Paris: OECD. http://www.oecd.org/dataoecd/51/8/ 1913021.pdf.

Otero, V., K.A. Meymaris, P. Ford, T. Garvin, D. Harlow, M. Reidel, B. Waite, and C. Mears. 2005. "Integrating Technology into Teacher Education: A Critical Framework for Implementing Reform." *Journal of Teacher Education* 56:8–23.

Parayil, G. 2005. "The Digital Divide and Increasing Returns: Contradictions of Informational Capitalism." *The Information Society* 21:41–51.

Robertson, H. 2003. "Toward a Theory of Negativity: Teacher Education and Information and Communications Technology." *Journal of Teacher Education* 54:280–96.

Russell, M., D. Bebell, L. O'Dwyer, and K. O'Connor. 2003. "Examining Teacher Technology Use: Implications for Preservice and Inservice Teacher Preparation." *Journal of Teacher Education* 54:297–310.

Sassen, S. 2002. "Towards a Sociology of Information Technology." *Current Sociology* 50:365–88.

Schon, A.D., B. Sanyal, and J.W. Mitchell. 2001. *High Technology and Low-Income Communities.* Cambridge: MIT Press.

Smith, E.D. 1987. *The Everyday World as Problematic.* Toronto: University of Toronto Press.

Snyder, I. 1998. *Beyond Page to Screen: Taking Literacy into the Electronic Era.* London: Routledge.

Statistics Canada. 2006. "The Daily: Canadian Internet Use Survey." *The Daily*. 15 August. http://www.statcan.ca/Daily/English/060815/d060815b.htm.

Thiessen, V. 2001. "Policy Research Issues for Canadian Youth: School–Work Transitions." Human Resources Development Canada. http://www.hrsdc.gc.ca/eng/cs/sp/hrsd/prc/publications/research/2001-000013/2001-000013.pdf.

Volman, M. and E. van Eck. 2001. "Gender Equity and Information Technology in Education: The Second Decade." *Review of Educational Research* 71:613–34.

Warschauer, M. 2002. "Reconceptualizing the Digital Divide." *First Monday* 7:10–17.

———. In press. "A Literacy Approach to the Digital Divide." In *Las mulialfabetizaciones en el espacio digital*, ed. M.A. Pereyra. Malaga, Spain: Ediciones Aljibe. http://www.gse.uci.edu/person/warschauer_m/docs/lit-approach.pdf.

Weinman, J. and P. Haag. 1999. "Gender Equity in Cyberspace." *Educational Leadership* 56:44–49.

Wotherspoon, Terry. 1998. *Sociology of Education in Canada: Critical Perspectives*. Toronto: Oxford University Press.

Young, J., C. Hall, and T. Clarke. 2007. "Challenges to University Autonomy in Initial Teacher Education Programmes: The Cases of England, Manitoba and British Columbia." *Teaching and Teacher Education* 23:81–93.

Chapter 6

Maybe it's not the teachers? Investigating the problem of ICT integration into education

E. Dianne Looker

Ted D. Naylor

Many researchers in education, particularly in the field of educational technology, argue that teachers are failing to leverage the potential offered by information and communication technologies (ICTs) for improving pedagogical practice (Brinkerhoff 2006; Cuckle, Clarke, and Jenkins et al. 2000). Generally, they contend that due to myriad reasons "true integration remains an elusive goal" (Maddux and Johnson 2005, 3). Much of this discussion focuses on why teachers and student teachers may or may not be successfully integrating technology into routine classroom use, and on identifying the barriers to full integration of technology into pedagogical practices. In this sense, teachers' attitudes and competence around technology are often presented as the final piece of the ICT education puzzle, needed to help youth build ICT knowledge and skill capacity (Cox, Webb, and Abbot 2003; Yoon, Ho, and Hedberg 2005). Cuckle et al. (2000, 337) observe that schools can only go so far to encourage ICT use, and that actual engagement depends on teachers' feelings, skills, and attitudes to ICT. Prior use of computers in teaching practices is also identified as essential to ICT integration in the classroom (Miller and Olson 1994). Concern has more recently, therefore, centred on how to ensure teachers and student teachers positively and actively orientate their teaching practice around the deep integration of ICTs (Kadijevich 2006; Leach and Moon 2000; Cuckle and Clarke 2002; Yoon et al. 2005). This is taken to involve moving beyond what researchers identify as "first-order" skills, which simply make traditional teaching more convenient or faster (Maddux and Johnson 2005), to having ICT integration facilitate the more transformative changes originally envisioned by its champions—changes touted in the educational policy and curriculum reform, and evidenced in high spending on ICT infrastructure at the school level.

Based on surveys completed by a non-representative sample of 119 Nova Scotia teachers and 141 second-year Faculty of Education student teachers, along with complementary qualitative data, this chapter wades into the discussions around teachers' attitudes and practices with respect to ICT integration. We argue that far from being resistant and/or without confidence in using a range of ICTs (Cox et al. 2003), teachers generally demonstrate positive attitudes toward technology and are open to using it in their classrooms. In this way, our findings problematize the implicit and taken-for-granted connections between ICTs and education typically found in the research literature. These studies tend to identify the teacher "problem" of ICT integration, and teachers' attitudes and skills with technology are routinely pointed to as the remaining obstacle to the apparently obvious benefits of a "transformative" ICT-integrated curriculum. Through an examination of our student-teacher and teacher data, we suggest that more critical attention needs to be focused on the key linkages between education and ICT in order to fully understand the complexity of ICT integration into the education system, particularly with respect to teachers' attitudes and practices. Through our empirical results, we tentatively question the ways in which "true ICT integration" can be seen as a discursive process that is acting to refashion the normative expectations and practices of teachers and their routine use of ICT. Cumulatively our data suggest that the barrier to deeper ICT integration within routine classroom practice may not be the teachers. Rather we contend that prior to a focus on teacher use and practice, what is required is a more systemic educational and pedagogical consensus around the links between ICTs, teaching practices, and educational outcomes, including post-secondary teacher training programs.

ICTs AND EDUCATION

A wide-ranging body of literature positions ICT integration as the key to transforming curriculum and pedagogical practices in education. A good deal of the literature from the past decade and earlier was coloured by optimistic claims that ICTs would fundamentally transform education for the better. As Bauer and Kenton (2005, 520) dramatically *under*state, "As a classroom tool, the computer has captured the attention of the education community." Calvert and Stacey (2003) claim that ICTs, or what they term "e-learning," should be embraced because it dramatically increases access to education itself and also allows for more "effective pedagogies." Becker (1994) characterizes exemplary use of ICT as a classroom environment that fully incorporates ICTs in the learning experience, resulting in intellectual growth rather than just the acquisition of a set of "isolated" technological skills. The premise is that home ICT use can be extended to the educational arena if educators understand the potential benefits and know how to leverage the appropriate strategies. Based on a series of case studies, Yoon et al. (2005, 145) argue that if teachers manage technology appropriately and receive adequate support, higher student involvement in learning is possible. The assumption in each characterization is that ICT integration, when used "effectively" by teachers, offers the possibility of engaged learning, in which the role of technology is to support the processes of student-led knowledge construction.[1] Appropriately, teaching as a practice is positioned as in need of transformative change, from traditional teacher-centred instruction to student-led computer-based instruction, through the design and wide implementation of technology-supported teacher-education programs (recommended by UNESCO 2002).

While far from exhaustive, this type of research is indicative of a stream of scholarship that closely links the integration of ICT to essential changes required in education—more broadly tied to the recognition that ICTs have become pervasive across socio-economic levels, as evidenced in popularized notions of the "networked" society, for example (see Castell 2000). Not surprisingly, then, there has been a strong push in public policy toward introducing ICTs into education. In Canada and abroad, ICTs continue to be touted as a transformative education curriculum and pedagogical tool. In terms of the former, educational curriculum reform embraces ICTs based on the rationale that the integration of information technology will positively support learning across the curriculum (Nova Scotia 2005; Milton 2003; OECD 2001). In terms of the latter, ICTs also continue to be positioned as a critical pedagogical tool for educators, one that can be used to support instruction and learning (Hughes 2005; Maddux and Johnson 2005). Student-teacher programs (Otero et al. 2005), professional development initiatives within education (Hughes 2005), and curriculum-reform developments (e.g., Nova Scotia 2005) persist in actively reorientating themselves around the "educational promise" that ICTs are taken to hold. In this context, future teachers (i.e., student teachers) and present teachers obviously form a key problematic in relation to "true" ICT integration within education. As Yoon et al. (2005, 155) contend, technology itself will not ensure there is a higher student involvement in learning, it is (supposedly) the teachers, their skills and their support that will lead to transformative ICT-based learning environments.

ICTs AND THE "PROBLEM" OF TEACHERS

Based on the contention that ICTs will have a positive impact on the educational system as a whole, coupled with a strong policy push from all provincial governments around introducing ICTs into the curriculum, the education system appears to have tackled the problem of access to ICTs for students and teachers. Researchers in the field of educational technology tend to group barriers to ICT integration into four general categories: resources, institutional and administrative support, training and experience, and attitudinal or personality factors. This chapter is primarily concerned with exploring and empirically evaluating the latter two factors.

The provincial Department of Education and the school boards in our sample have clearly placed a high priority on ICTs, and we cautiously suggest that a significant degree of institutional and administrative support exists for teachers in relation to their use of ICTs. In Nova Scotia, the Department of Education has created a "Learning Resources and Technology" division, for example, and each school board typically has a technology administrator responsible for overseeing and supporting technology initiatives within schools and classrooms. This general assessment is supported by other studies that suggest we are moving past the "problem" of hardware, and thus "current attention has turned to what is actually happening in the classroom with computer technology" (Bauer and Kenton 2005, 520). Although there is no dollar figure available for ICT investment in Canadian public schools, the figure is undoubtedly high. Canada is ranked among the highest in the world when it comes to computer and Internet access, with an estimated one million computers in schools nationwide, and approximately 90% of these connected to the Internet (Statistics Canada 2002, 2004a). The Programme for International Student Assessment (PISA), comparing thirty-one OECD countries, demonstrates that Canada is above average in student-to-computer ratios, percentage of school computers connected to the Internet, and computer availability at home (Statistics Canada 2004b). Focus has therefore turned to examining the practices of teachers with ICTs in an effort to double back and reassess the question of why ICTs are still so under-utilized in classroom settings, if they are used at all, and why the initial educational promises held by ICTs have not yet materialized: "students still spend most of their school day as if these tools and information resources had never been invented" (Becker 1998, quoted in Bauer and Kenton 2005, 520).

Research suggests that ICT integration into the classroom is strongly mediated by the beliefs of teachers and the value they place on ICTs (Bransford & Schwartz 1999). Cox et al. (2003, 27) contend that "the beliefs which teachers have about the power and scope of ICT, its new modes of knowledge representation and therefore the different ways in which pupils learn, will profoundly affect the affordances controlling the learning actions and activities." The training of teachers at the post-secondary level is, therefore, one crucial factor in any successful implementation of ICT into the classroom setting (Kadijevich 2006). The degree to which both student teachers and current classroom teachers report comfort with ICTs and their acceptance and overall attitudes toward ICT use are therefore important factors in helping us gain a better picture of whether teachers remain an obstacle to ICT integration. Notably research to date suggests that ICT integration is *not* occurring within classroom settings, either as an instructional delivery tool or as an element of curriculum itself. Although it is clear that the presence of technology in classrooms has increased overall in education, this presence is not really surprising given the emphasis on ensuring access to ICTs by government and policy-makers alike.

Appropriately, the first generation of research around access to ICTs largely conceptualized equitable ICT access as a problem of infrastructure. To this end, wide-scale investments were made, and equitable access to ICTs is no longer an issue at the forefront of Canadian policy-makers.

As suggested above, the emphasis has moved to a closer examination of the actual uses, or lack thereof, of ICTs in the classroom. Again, this concern mirrors a broader collection of research that now attempts to understand the notion of a digital divide in more complex terms (Parayil 2005), emphasizing the need to also pay attention to the actual contextual uses of technology. Education researchers now find themselves wading deeper into an exploration of why most teachers are not using ICTs in the ways originally imagined and intended. In this respect, these second-generation studies are more revealing and problematic when it comes to the links between teachers and ICT integration, since the overall finding has been that ICT use is largely confined to "low-level" tasks, such as word processing and using the Internet. Studies in both the U.S. and abroad suggest the same: that use of ICT is relatively low and is focused on a fairly narrow range of ICTs. As Ertmer (2005, 26) observes, "Thus, while instructional computer use appears to be increasing (at least measured by self-report data), the most common and frequent uses have resulted in only incremental, or first-order, changes in teacher style and remain far removed from the best practices advocated in the literature." When we consider these developments, and the lingering gap between rhetoric and reality, in relation to our discussion about the importance of teacher attitudes, beliefs and routine use to ICT integration on the behalf of teachers, we are undoubtedly left with a question of why teachers appear to be so poorly utilizing ICTs within their classrooms. In other words, if full ICT integration is now dependent upon teachers and, by extension, future teachers' attitudes toward and uses of ICT, then, admittedly, we are left with the assumption that teachers remain the "problem" with respect to ICT integration with education.

DATA SOURCES

In order to address these issues we examine surveys that were distributed to all teachers in schools participating in the Equity and Technology project. From the ten schools in Nova Scotia, 119 Nova Scotia teachers completed the survey. Within three Nova Scotia faculties of education at the post-secondary level, 141 second-year Faculty of Education student teachers completed surveys. Thirteen interviews were conducted with faculty from these three schools. Ten interviews were conducted with second-year Bachelor of Education students, and three interviews were conducted with members from the education community from Nova Scotia to provide additional context and insight into the issues under exploration. Additionally, six separate focus groups with second-year students were conducted at two faculties of education. Second-year students were explicitly targeted because, in accordance with the degree requirements of the department, each student would have had the opportunity to complete an in-class practicum teaching in a classroom setting, providing additional insights and experiences that first-year students could not add.

FINDINGS

The first issue we examine is the use of ICT by the responding teachers. Table 6.1 shows the relevant results.

As we can see, the only activities that these teachers report using in class "to facilitate student learning" with any regularity are word processing and the Internet. Less than half of the teachers report using any of the other activities more than once a month in class. These findings echo research undertaken around ICT integration in classroom use by teachers, where teachers primarily are found to use ICT for low-level tasks (word processing and the Internet), while higher level use is still very low (Bauer and Kenton 2005). Others observe that many of the positive attitudes toward ICTs reported by teachers in survey data are rooted in educators understanding the instructional implications of the Internet as an information and search resource (Anderson and Speck 2001). Taken together these findings confirm that teachers are not using technology in ways advocated in the literature concerning ICT integration and teaching practice and use (Ertmer 2005).

As we can see from Table 6.2, teachers use ICT for other tasks at a somewhat higher rates than those reported in Table 6.1. However, the tasks described are still fairly straightforward: using the Internet to get information, school administrative tasks (such as timetabling and grade calculation), or emailing others. Other data show that only about a third (36%) have a class website and even fewer (18%) have a personal website. There is little evidence here of what most ICT educational literature would describe as "deep integration" of ICT

TABLE 6.1

Use of ICT by teachers in class for student learning

ICT activity	At least a few times a week (%)	A few times a month (%)	Less than once a month (%)
Word processing	58	18	24
Internet	47	33	20
Email	37	10	54
Graphics	36	13	51
Curriculum specific software	22	14	64
Presentation software	20	24	57
CD-ROM/online encyclopedia	12	20	68
Spreadsheets	8	16	76

TABLE 6.2

Teacher use of ICT for other tasks

ICT activity	At least a few times a week (%)	A few times a month (%)	Less than once a month (%)
Use Internet to get information	68	20	12
Use Internet for other reasons	76	21	3
School administrative tasks	62	19	20
Email other teachers	60	19	22
Email family or friends	59	14	27
Prepare computer presentations for class	35	22	43
Search online catalogue or CD-ROM data base	11	27	62

into the curriculum or routine pedagogical use. Deep integration implies the possibility that ICT can be routinely embedded in constructivist pedagogy and employed to transform and change students' learning routines, cognitive processes, and problem solving in the classroom (Hughes 2005, 281).

Interpreting our data in relation to a consideration of variable ICT integration within classrooms, the use patterns evident in our findings do not necessarily mean that teachers are resisting ICT. Overall, as Table 6.3 shows, these teachers have positive attitudes to ICT.

The vast majority of the teachers say they enjoy using computers and feel these technologies make teaching easier. Computers help them meet the needs of particular students. They like courses where they get to use computers. Very few (less than a third) find computers frustrating. Even fewer say they are nervous about using computers. In other data (not shown) 78% say computers have a positive effect on student learning, and 55% agree they have a positive effect on student creativity. There is no suggestion here that teacher attitudes to ICT are a barrier to ICT integration. While low-level technology uses may be associated with teacher-centred practices (Becker 1994), our findings suggest that low-level uses do not necessarily correlate with poor or negative attitudes to ICTs. Moreover these positive attitudes are echoed by those who are preparing to enter the teaching profession, as indicated by Table 6.4. When we ask student teachers in about their attitudes to ICT we do not see a marked difference from those reported by current teachers.

TABLE 6.3
Teacher attitudes to ICT

	Agree (%)	Neutral (%)	Disagree (%)
I enjoy using a computer	87	3	9
Computers make teaching easier	83	6	11
Computers help me address the needs of particular students	74	9	16
I like courses that use computers	69	8	23
Technology helps me accommodate different learning styles	65	20	15
Lot of pressure to use ICT	45	22	33
Using a computer frustrates me	30	3	67
ICT requires too much technical knowledge	17	14	69
Working with computers makes me nervous	11	6	83
I'd avoid a course with computers	9	7	84

TABLE 6.4
Student teacher attitudes to ICT

	Agree (%)	Neutral (%)	Disagree (%)
I enjoy using a computer	94	3	3
Computers make teaching easier	86	7	7
I like courses that use computers	78	12	10
Lot of pressure to use ICT	46	43	12
Using a computer frustrates me	20	9	72
ICT requires too much technical knowledge	6	17	78
Working with computers makes me nervous	6	6	88
I'd avoid a course with computers	4	8	88

If we compare Table 6.3 and Table 6.4, we see only a slight difference in that more current than future teachers agree that a computer can be frustrating. Interestingly more current teachers *dis*agree that there is a lot of pressure for teachers to use ICT. These tables document that not only is the problem *not* with teacher attitudes to ICT but also that the solution for deeper ICT integration is not simply to wait until younger teachers replace those currently in the classroom. This has important implications for researchers who posit that increased or prolonged technology use will eventually prompt teachers to change their classroom practices to more constructivist approaches, a position that frames much of the policy discourse and infrastructure investments made around ICT investment in education.

While some large-scale surveys on computer use paint a bleak picture of teacher competence with ICTs for classroom use (U.S. Department of Education 2003), our survey results suggest that teachers in our sample are fairly knowledgeable about computers and ICT. Almost three quarters (73%) report they have been using computers for ten years or more. In terms of their self-assessed competence levels, the mean level on a scale of 1 (very low) to 7 (expert) is 4.6; 60% report a level 5 or better. In other words, they not only have been using computers for a decade or more, they see themselves as fairly competent. Student teachers report similar levels of expertise—an average score of 5.1 on the seven-point scale. Collectively these findings suggest that the problem may not be the connection between teachers and ICTs. Rather, the problem of ICT integration may be more complex in terms of the links assumed between ICTs, teachers' use of ICTs and education as a whole, an observation we consider more fully in the next section.

In terms of training, the vast majority of responding teachers (87%) report some formal training in ICT in the last five years. Most (58%) list two or more types of formal training. Most frequent is training offered through their respective school boards as well as provincial department of education in-services. Informal training is also mentioned by 67% of the teachers. Nevertheless, 63% say they would take additional training if it were available to them. So, these teachers are fairly knowledgeable, they have used computers for some time and feel comfortable with them, and they see computers and ICT as facilitating their teaching. Where are the barriers?

In Table 6.5, teachers report a number of concerns and suggestions about what they would need to integrate ICT more effectively into their teaching.

TABLE 6.5

Teacher-reported needs to use ICT more effectively in classes

Need to use ICT more effectively	Yes (%)	Don't know (%)	No (%)
More opportunities to work with colleagues using ICT	79	7	15
More resources on how to integrate ICT into the curriculum	77	5	18
More curriculum based software	75	9	15
More computers for students	74	5	21
More technical support	71	10	19
More powerful computers	70	11	20
More training	67	7	26
Faster Internet connections	49	10	41
More access to the Internet	46	12	42
More compelling reasons to incorporate ICT	42	10	49

Although the findings above indicate that teachers feel comfortable with ICT, it is clear that they feel they need a range of supports to incorporate it more thoroughly into their classroom teaching. The fact that such a high percentage agree they could use more opportunities to work with colleagues using technology-enhanced curriculum units suggests many teachers feel isolated in terms of developing ways to integrate ICT in their classes. This result is consistent with the qualitative data, in which many respondents reported that they felt isolated in developing ICT skill. Many of those who reported that they were at the most expert level felt they were carrying the load; they would like others to share it, and to share experiences and ideas with. This result is also consistent with responses to another question (not shown), where less than half (43%) agree that their school colleagues discuss their use of ICT. Table 6.5 also shows that teachers report needing more resources on *how* to integrate technology into the curriculum as well as more curriculum-based software. Nevertheless, overall our findings suggest that it could be important to revisit the assumed links between ICTs and education given the evidence to date on its integration in routine classroom use.

TABLE 6.6

Teacher concerns with ICT

	A concern (%)
Plagiarism from the web	91
Student frustration with ICT	62
Outdated or unavailable Internet resources	59
Pornography	59
Distraction from other aspects of the course	57
Identity theft	42
Increased performance expectations	41

Less than half of the teachers in our survey report that they need more or faster access to the Internet. Less than half say they need more compelling reasons to incorporate technology into their courses. To more fully integrate ICT into classroom use, teachers report that what they need is guidance and resources to assist them to take the next step.[2] They also report a need for technical support. Over 70% say they need more technical support to work effectively with ICT. In another question (not shown) only about a third (36%) agree that ICT equipment gets fixed quickly when it breaks down.

In other data almost two-thirds of teachers say their school has a policy to use ICT across the curriculum; however, there is little evidence that these policies have been effectively implemented. What is more, over a quarter (28%) say they don't know if their school has such a policy.

Teachers do have some concerns that may inhibit their use of ICT. As Table 6.6 shows, chief among these are concerns about plagiarism. Also of concern are student levels of frustration with ICT, outdated or unavailable resources, and pornography. Over half the teachers also have concerns about ICT distracting students from other components of a course. This concern reflects the findings that suggest that ICT is not well integrated across the curriculum, so it serves as a distraction rather than an integral part of course work.

DISCUSSION

Overall, our findings paint a contradictory and nuanced picture. The data suggest that teachers report positive attitudes, high levels of competence with

ICTs, and a considerably long time using ICTs (73% of teachers for ten years or more). At the same time, use of ICTs is confined to tasks such as word processing, administration tasks, and using the Internet. That said, teachers do routinely use ICTs and are neither "nervous" of nor "frustrated" by the technology. In fact, they openly welcome opportunities to train with ICTs more and to develop a range of supports to incorporate it more thoroughly into their classroom teaching. At the post-secondary level, student teachers report similarly high levels of competence with ICTs and positive attitudes toward ICTs. These findings support what Hughes (2005) notes, that currently teachers use ICTs in ways that sustain rather than innovate current pedagogy. The question remains, then, for many researchers (Bauer and Kenton 2005; Mumtaz 2000; Hughes 2005; Ertmer 2005), why is the uptake of ICT by teachers so slow and seemingly confined to low-level tasks?

We believe that part of the answer to this question lies in our results, which indicate the need for a more nuanced consideration of how teachers actually use ICTs. How teachers use ICT in practice is too often evaluated against a more conceptual agenda, led by educational researchers, to refashion education through technology to a constructivist pedagogical paradigm. In other words, we contend that much of the focus on the teacher "problem" of ICT integration is rooted in a wider assumption that latently assumes ICTs are agents to more fundamental changes in the educational system and pedagogical practices generally. Thus, what is getting lost amid the push to integrate ICT into education is an empirical appreciation and understanding of the *actual uses* of technology teachers employ to cope with the day-to-day demands of their classrooms. When we consider the findings in Chapter 5, which concludes that faculties of education have done a poor job of identifying a common or even core base of ICT competency for student teachers, then an evaluation of how current teachers are "failing" to leverage the potential offered by ICTs to transform teaching practice appears, at best, premature.

Although our findings articulate a range of potential teacher needs that might result in more effective use of ICTs, there is no clear evidence that "more" of everything will lead to improved educational outcomes for students or teachers, let alone the transformative changes envisioned by many educational researchers. As Cuban, Kirkpatrick, and Peck (2001, 825) note, based on their results of a study of two high-tech high schools in California, "Few fundamental changes in the dominant mode of teacher-centred instruction had occurred ... Even in computer-based classes, teacher-centered instruction was the norm." Evidence from our data confounds the assumptions between ICT integration and transformative teaching practices even further. A respondent from one of our student-teacher focus groups observes about their practicum experience, "I find when you give students computer time ... it's really hard for them to take it seriously even ... to stay on task, and that's the part I find about it that's more of a hassle sometimes." Although teacher pedagogical beliefs may be seen as the "final frontier" for ICT integration (Ertmer 2005, 1), the assumption that ICT is necessarily linked to a trajectory of a more student-centred constructivist pedagogy for classroom teachers is questionable in light of the findings reported here.

In attempting to untangle some of the contradictions raised by our findings, namely that teachers appear positive about and competent with ICT yet do not use it for what educational researchers would term "higher," "deeper," or "second-order" uses, it is helpful to consider the notion of ICT literacy. In a Canadian schooling context, the apparent requirements of a "knowledge economy" have led to a renewed emphasis on increasing the current knowledge and skills of students. Schools, education authorities, and the public at-large place a high priority on literacy, which has led to an increased focus by educators at all levels on promoting, measuring, and improving literacy and, correspondingly, student performance (Sim 2006). The push around ICT integration is partly, then, a question of values about what teachers should be teaching and how they should be teaching. As the Nova Scotia Department of Education states, the context of students' ICT use is that "lifelong learning and employment in the information economy demand fluency and critical engagement with new media texts ... Through the influence of ICT, Nova Scotian learners have the opportunity to access, use, and augment human knowledge more quickly and comprehensively than ever before" (Nova Scotia 2005, 5, 7). If ICT is the "new" literacy, then student teachers and current teachers are presumed to be at the heart of ensuring this transformative change. As Watson (2001, 251) notes, "IT is not only perceived as a catalyst for change, but also a change in teaching style, change in learning approaches, and a change in access to information." And a principal in a Nova Scotia high school contends, "We need better ways of incorporating technology into the program. I'm not sure how much, actually, training (new teachers) are getting related to technology and delivering the program." We are left yet again wondering how to make sense of this apparent paradox: that ICT is seen as increasingly crucial to learning and education, but apparently it is not being effectively incorporated into curriculum programs within schools, classrooms, and teacher-training programs.

The contradictions in our findings suggest that as the definition of literacy continues to shift beyond being reading and writing to more nuanced skills around ICT literate practices, the current proliferation of skills and tools that are being described as "ICT-related" makes it exceedingly difficult to pin down what ICT literacy is taken to mean, particularly as it relates to education. This suggests, in part, a reason why everyone can report to be positive toward it, be competent with it, but not use it in their pedagogical practices. The fact that the teachers in our sample simultaneously rate their competence as high and their attitudes positive, and yet respond equally positively for more training opportunities, suggests a critical systemic gap in understanding what ICT integration actually means for routine pedagogy. Although respondents in our sample report ICT use at what educational researchers deem "low-order," the qualitative component of our research reveals that this characterization of ICT integration could be misleading. As one of our current teacher respondents observes: "You know, I can't imagine—it's hard to remember what it was like before. I mean now, you come in, turn on the computer, check today's announcements, get up your attendance program, to have in an instant how a student is doing, print off an individual student report ... I find this a very powerful tool for students and for parents too, and for myself."

While this use of ICT is "confined" to an administrative function, the integration of ICT here is seen and understood by the teacher as not only helpful but "powerful" for his day-to-day pedagogical routine in the classroom. It is therefore important for any analysis or policy initiative around ICT integration to recognize that there are important differences in use, skill levels, and objectives in using ICTs throughout the social order, including within the field of education. The difficulty in understanding ICT integration is that there is yet to be an agreed-on consensus about what ICT integration actually *is*, including at the post-secondary training level. In short, conflating ICT integration with constructivist pedagogy and transformative change may be obscuring important uses and routine changes taking place within what critics would characterize as the "status quo." Another current teacher respondent observes: "I can specialize more because I have things done. Case in point here ... when I went to start my first day, my first class walked in, and as they were coming in the doors, (I) felt this great whoosh of anxiety. I'm not ready. I'm not ready, and I just looked over at my computer, and I opened the folder, grade eight whatever, grade eight session one, and course intro, lesson one, click, click, and we were off."

Here we find a teacher using the computer as an archive, certainly not a "higher-order" function indicative of transformative student-centred learning. ICT integration here amounts to a mundane and a supportive function serving routine functions of a classroom teacher.

CONCLUSION

A key finding of this study, then, is that there are not necessarily "higher-order" users of technology and "lower-order" users of technology when considering how individuals employ ICTs in ways that matter to their teaching lives, circumstances, and needs. Given this caveat, ICT integration needs to be more loosely conceptualized as a range of classroom strategies that potentially improve the educational experience, as opposed to existing along a set of ever-spiralling competencies of ICT expertise. "Expertise is individual in nature and has strong roots in the individual's interest and motivation," observe Ilomaki and Rantanen (2007, 133). At the same time, and recognizing the explicit lack of a systemic and empirical consensus around the ability of ICT to transform pedagogical practices, there needs to be a wider appreciation for the many ways ICTs are *actively* and *positively* being used by teachers. Dexter, Anderson, and Becker (1999) note that teachers can choose within the norms of teaching practice what works for them, allowing them to adopt, adapt, or reject instructional technique and/or reform. That so many teachers are rejecting fundamental pedagogical changes envisioned by champions of ICT integration, favouring instead incremental use and change that matters to their actual classroom strategies and routines, should serve notice to those hoping to transform the educational system through the integration of ICT alone.

This chapter speaks directly to the scholarship and assumptions that categorically claim, "There can be no debate about the reality of e-learning; in spite of concerns that many may have, it is growing and flourishing at all levels" (Calvert and Stacy 2003, 51). Overall, our findings seek to problematize the assumptions around ICT integration into classroom settings, particularly the popular assessment that if only teachers knew how to use technology better, then the true benefits of ICTs in schools would be unleashed for all students. Our data suggests most teachers are perfectly comfortable using technology and have been doing so for extended periods of time. In this way, we caution against assumptions around poor teacher ICT literacy and its supposed connection to poor ICT integration.

It is worth noting that fields such as the sociology of work have historically documented the tendency for technology to degrade and simplify sites of work (Braverman 1974; Zuboff 1989), where the introduction of technology is seen to have potentially negative consequences for labour. When we consider that most of the technological applications are corporate creations and/or professional based tools,[3] we suggest that teachers are perhaps strategically adopting only the most useful components of ICTs in relation to their individuals needs and understanding. Further, the claim that students may know "more" about some components of the technology and feel more comfortable with it is irrelevant to the educational goals of the schools if these students are primarily using computers as toys and entertainment devices. It falls to the teachers, not the students, to ensure that ICT is used in pedagogically appropriate ways. We conclude, then, that teachers' continued reports of positive attitudes and routine uptake of ICTs in their classrooms indicate that ICT integration is taking place *despite* how technology is being positioned in relation to education by both the educational community and many proponents who decry the lack of ICT use by teachers in their classrooms.

Based on their responses and our observations in the schools, it is clear we need to move beyond the assumption that the presence of ICT and/or teachers' familiarity with it will somehow magically transform either the curriculum or pedagogical techniques. Teachers need institutional supports to effect any such transformation: more educational software adapted to a curriculum that incorporates and builds on the unique multimedia capabilities that are built into some of the new technologies; structures that facilitate their interaction with others using this technology; and institutional practices put in place that help identify, share, and somehow institutionalize some of the incredibly innovative practices using ICT that are taking place in the classroom. Teachers need to be recognized as being part of the solution rather than the problem.

NOTES

1   This type of learning is often termed constructivist styled pedagogy, associated with learning theorist Jean Piaget (1967). At the most general level, this approach understands teachers as facilitators to learning, where the "learner" plays an active role in the content, and learning is reciprocal, intuitive and collaboratively based.
2   Student teachers in the faculties of education report are even more likely than current teachers to emphasize the need for more curriculum-based software; 91% of the student teachers, compared to 75% of current teachers, say this is important if they are to incorporate ICT effectively in their classes.
3   For example, Photoshop's website states that this product is "ideal" for "professional photographers, serious amateur photographers, graphic designers, and web designers" (see http://www.adobe.com/products/photoshop/index.html).

WORKS CITED

Anderson, R.S. and B.W. Speck. 2001. *Using Technology in K–8 Literacy Classrooms.* Upper Saddle River, NJ: Merrill Prentice-Hall.

Bauer, J. and J. Kenton. 2005. "Toward Technology Integration in the Schools: Why It Isn't Happening." *Journal of Technology and Teacher Education* 13:519–46.

Becker, H.J. 1994. "How Exemplary Computer-using Teachers Differ from Other Teachers: Implications for Realizing the Potential of Computers in Schools." *Journal of Research on Computing in Education* 26:291–321.

Bransford, J.D. and D.L. Schwartz. 1999. "Rethinking Transfer: A Simple Proposal with Multiple Implications." In *Review of Research in Education*, ed. G. P. Baxter, A. Iran-Nejad, and P.D. Pearson, 61–101. Washington, DC: American Educational Research Association.

Braverman, H. 1974. *Labor and Monopoly Capital.* New York: Monthly Review Press.

Brinkerhoff, J. 2006. "Effects of a Long-Duration, Professional Development Academy on Technology Skills, Computer Self-Efficacy, and Technology Integration Beliefs and Practices." *International Society for Technology in Education* 39:22–43.

Calvert, T. and P. Stacey. 2003. "Learning for an e-Connected World." In *The e-Connected World: Risks and Opportunities*, ed. S. Coleman, 51–68. Montreal: McGill-Queen's University Press.

Castell, M. 2000. *The Rise of the Network Society*, 2nd edition. Malden, MA: Blackwell.

Cox, M., M. Webb, and C. Abbot. 2003. "ICT and Pedagogy: A Review of the Research Literature." British Communications and Technology Agency.

Cuban, L., H. Kirkpatrick, and C. Peck. 2001. "High Access and Low Use of Technology in High School Classrooms: Explaining an Apparent Paradox." *American Educational Research Journal* 38:813–34.

Cuckle, P., S. Clarke, and I. Jenkins. 2000. "Students' Information and Communications Technology Skills and Their Use during Teaching Training." *Journal of Information Technology for Teacher Education* 9:9–22.

Cuckle, P. and S. Clarke. 2002. "Mentoring Student Teachers in Schools: Views, Practices and Access to ICT." *Journal of Computer Assisted Learning* 18:330–40.

Dexter, L.D., R.E. Anderson, and J.H. Becker. 1999. "Teachers' Views of Computers as Catalysts for Changes in Their Teaching Practices." *Journal of Research Computing in Education* 31:221–39.

Department of Education [U.S.], Office of the Under Secretary, Policy and Program Studies Service. 2003. *Federal Funding for Educational Technology and How It Is Used in the Classroom: A Summary of Findings from the Integrated Studies of Educational Technology.* Washington, DC.

Ertmer, A.P. 2005. "Teacher Pedagogical Beliefs: The Final Frontier in Our Quest for Technology Integration?" *Educational Technology Research and Development* 53:25–39.

Hughes, J. 2005. "The Role of Teacher Knowledge and Learning Experiences in Forming Technology-Integrated Pedagogy." *Journal of Technology and Teacher Education* 13:277–302.

Ilomaki, L. and P. Rantanen. 2007. "Intensive Use of ICT in School: Developing Differences in Students' ICT Expertise." *Computers in Education* 48:119–36.

Kadijevich, D. 2006. "Achieving Educational Technology Standards: The Relationship between Student Teacher's Interest and Institutional Support Offered." *Journal of Computer Assisted Learning* 22:437–43.

Leach, J. and B. Moon. 2000. "Pedagogy, Information and Communications Technology and Teachers' Professional Knowledge." *The Curriculum Journal* 11:385–404.

Maddux, D.C. and D.J. Lamont. 2005. "Information Technology, Type II Classroom Integration, and the Limited Infrastructure in Schools." *Computers in the Schools* 22:1–5.

Miller, L. and J. Olson. 1994. "Putting the Computer in Its Place: A Study of Teaching with Technology." *Journal of Curriculum Studies* 26:121–41.

Milton, P. 2003, "Trends in the Integration of ICT and Learning in K–12 Systems." Toronto, ON: Canadian Education Association. http://www.cea-ace.ca/media/en/Trends_ICT_Integration.pdf.

Mumtaz, S. 2000. "Technology, Pedagogy and Education." *Journal of Information Technology for Teacher Education* 9:319–41.

Organization for Economic Co-operation and Development. 1996. "The Knowledge-based Economy." http://www.oecd.org/dataoecd/51/8/1913021.pdf.

Otero, V., K.A. Meymaris, P. Ford, T. Garvin, D. Harlow, M. Reidel, et al. 2005. "Integrating Technology into Teacher Education: A Critical Framework for Implementing Reform." *Journal of Teacher Education* 56:8–23.

Parayil, G. 2005. "The Digital Divide and Increasing Returns: Contradictions of Informational Capitalism." *The Information Society* 21:41–51.

Nova Scotia. 2005. "Survey of Classroom Computers in Nova Scotia Schools." Nova Scotia Department of Education.

Sim, A. 2006. "An Investigation of the Literacy Demands and Support Given to a Year 8 Class." *Australian Journal of Language and Literacy* 29:240–51.

Statistics Canada. 2002. "The Daily." 29 October. http://www.statcan.ca/Daily/English/021029/d021029a.htm.

———. 2004a. "The Daily." 10 June. http://www.statcan.ca/Daily/English/040610/d040610b.htm.

———. 2004b. "Computers in the Classroom: Opportunity and Challenge." Statistics Canada, Education Matters. http://www.statcan.gc.ca/pub/81-004-x/200409/7017-eng.htm.

UNESCO. 2002. *Information and Communication Technologies in Teacher Education: A Planning Guide.* http://unesdoc.unesco.org/images/0012/001295/129533e.pdf.

Watson, M. Deryn. 2001. "Pedagogy before Technology: Re-thinking the Relationship between ICT and Teaching." *Education and Information Technology* 6:251–66.

Yoon, S.F., J. Ho, and G.J. Hedberg. 2005. "Teachers as Designers of Learning Environments." *Computers in the Schools* 22:145–57.

Zuboff, S. 1984. *In the Age of the Smart Machine.* New York: Basic Books.

Chapter 7

"Being hooked up": Exploring the experiences of street youth and information technologies

Jeff Karabanow

Ted D. Naylor

The vast majority of research with street youth has focused on etiology and street culture (Karabanow 2004; Panter-Brick and Smith 2000; Raffaelli and Larson 1999; Robertson and Greenblatt 1992). Such investigations have been concerned with how young people enter street life and the myriad of activities associated with street survival (see for example, Green 1998; Karabanow et al. 2005; McCarthy 1990; Michaud 1988; Raffaelli and Larson 1999). This chapter takes a different, yet complimentary, approach and explores the experiences of twenty Halifax street youth with regard to information and communication technologies (ICTs). For the purposes of this study, ICTs primarily refer to the basic networking possibilities created through the Internet and the prerequisite computer skills required for "being online."

The significance of such an investigation is twofold. One, such an investigation recognizes that, at present, many aspects of civil society incorporate diverse elements of ICTs in ways that are thought to be novel, potentially creating new possibilities of social capital in terms of bonding, solidifying, or enhancing existing relationships among communities, groups, or individuals. Paradoxically, at the same time, the lack of skills and competency with ICTs, coupled with inequalities around access for marginalized populations, may only deepen feelings of isolation and social exclusion (Looker and Thiessen, 2003; Eamon 2004). This is particularly poignant for street youth, who are by nature a marginalized population and are found to suffer from loneliness differently from those in the general population (Rokach 2005, 477).

Secondly, there is now a significant contention that literacy with ICTs is fundamental to a successful socio-economic sphere in an age of "informational capitalism" (Parayil 2005), or what is commonly referred to as a "knowledge economy." Competency with ICTs, therefore, is considered to be increasingly essential for social capital in terms of its bridging capacity, potentially creating access to education and skills training programs, and for labour-force participation (Eng 1994; Murray 1995; Pearson 2002). As Milton (2003, 2) notes, "ICT skills are a key factor in both individuals' success in the labour market and in national economic growth." When we consider that many homeless and at-risk youth lack basic employment skills (Karabanow et al. 2005) and also comprise a marginalized and vulnerable population in relation to civil society at large, exploring street youth experiences and attitudes in relation to ICTs becomes an important field of empirical inquiry. Nevertheless, there continues to be a dearth of knowledge concerning ICTs and homeless populations.

This study begins to explore how young people living on the street in one Canadian city understand, experience, and access ICTs. Equally important, the study also attempts to shed light on whether street youth feel "hooked up" or "left behind," embedded within the tensions of living on the margins of an increasingly technology-driven socio-economic landscape.

YOUTH, STREET LIFE, AND ACADEMIC STUDY

One of the significant findings from this study suggests that young people living on the street and/or in emergency shelters and supportive housing structures are not only familiar and comfortable with ICTs but interact with this technology frequently. The remarkable issue here is that these young people are primarily homeless and spend much of their day-to-day living attempting to satisfy basic needs such as food, shelter, and safety.

The majority of research about street youth has focused on the ways in which these young people enter street life and experience homeless culture. There has always been a debate within the literature as to the "true" causes of homelessness, some conceptualizing the phenomenon in terms of "running toward" the glamour, freedom, and excitement of street life (Yablonsky 1968), others as pathologies inherent within the actor such as "runaway reaction disorders" (Stierlin 1973) and "depressed-withdrawn delinquencies" (Edelbrock

1980). In the last few decades, especially considering the discovery of high levels of sexual and physical abuse experienced in street youth populations (Janus et al. 1987; Kufeldt and Nimmo 1987), the conceptualization of street entry has been understood in terms of "running away" from traumatic and distressful experiences within the family unit, child welfare settings, and other institutional structures, such as school. Numerous studies concerned with street etiology have pointed toward family dysfunction and strain, problematic child welfare experiences, poverty-related living, struggles with sexual orientation, school dropouts, and substance abuse (Child Welfare League of America 1991; Green 1998; Karabanow 2004; McCarthy 1990; Morrissette and McIntyre 1989). In general, it has become more apparent that homeless youth face grave situations prior to street life and move toward the street as a way to manage and cope with traumatic situations (Karabanow 2008). As one young person living on the street in Toronto remarked, "Don't you think I'd go back [to family] if I could, why would someone want to be out here on the streets?" (Karabanow 2003). It is apparent that many young people perceive the street as safer than where they have come from—a telling point considering the dangers and exploitation of street living. The "street-as-dangerous" understanding of homeless youth effectively underscores the current study and how we understand homeless youths' interaction and engagement of ICTs.

Street life presents a myriad of activities, legal/quasi-legal and illegal, to occupy the time and energy of its inhabitants. Much has been written about the degradation and exploitation of young people on the street, primarily in terms of the drug and sex trade, unsanitary living conditions (in squats, sidewalks, under bridges, and in parks), risks to physical and mental health, and issues of violence and abuse. Although there has been some attention paid to the sense of communities or surrogate families that emerge on the street, the vast majority of street experiences appear to be degrading, unsafe, and traumatic. The majority of young people on the street engage in informal employment, such as panhandling and squeegeeing, to earn a meagre income. Moreover, many street youth are involved with drug selling and prostitution. A minority of the population does seek out formal employment (such as in the restaurant and construction business), especially those who have a stable living arrangement such as a long-term shelter or supportive housing structure. The vast majority of street youth do not maintain ties to school; however, some do attend alternative school programs that are supportive of their street lifestyle (Fitzgerald 1998).

CONTEXTUALIZING THE DISCUSSION — STREET YOUTH
IN HALIFAX

According to the *Portraits of Streets and Shelters* studies conducted by Halifax Regional Municipality in 2003 and 2004, one-third of the homeless population in Metro Halifax, Nova Scotia, is under the age of twenty-four (Halifax Regional Municipality 2004; 2005). Two recent investigations of street life in Halifax (Karabanow et al. 2005; Karabanow 2004) found that young people on the street described themselves as not having a choice to stay at home. Most youth had experienced turbulent family backgrounds, often characterized by severe physical, sexual, and/or emotional abuse and neglect. Life on the street for the vast majority of youth was described as lonely, dangerous, unhealthy, and detrimental to their sense of personal identity. Many homeless youth were struggling with economic, social, and health-related problems associated with street life. Youth highlighted the extreme difficulty of finding/keeping formal employment and/or maintaining a school schedule and staying focused on their studies while being homeless. Most of the youth interviewed envisioned and craved a conventional lifestyle. For the majority, governmental and non-governmental services were inadequate in providing required supports (i.e., there were too few services available to them). What these youth desire most is long-term, safe, and affordable places to live.

As with other subcultures, the culture of street life is diverse and complex. As such, those who make up street or homeless youth are equally diverse in terms of background, present experiences, and future aspirations. Labels such as "squeegee kids," "punks," "street-entrenched," "group-home," "in-and-outers," "runaways," or "shelter youth" are used in the literature as an attempt to make sense of the population and to organize analytical discussions (see, for example, Kufeldt and Nimmo 1987; McCarthy 1990; Morrisette and McIntyre 1989; Shane 1989; van der Ploeg 1989). This study has made every effort not to construct labels in order to acknowledge the diversity of street youth populations. Not only are such monikers static and vague, but life on the streets is extremely ephemeral, so the meaning of these categories may be different depending on the circumstance in which the youth finds him—or herself.

Homeless youth are by nature a transient population, frequently moving between and within localities in search of supportive services, basic needs, adventure, a sense of community, and better (real and perceived) opportunities (Karabanow 2004). Not surprisingly, youth homelessness is also extremely complex, not only because of the diversity of the population but also because of the challenges in defining, describing, and understanding street etiology, street culture, and most important, the individuals who make up the "street youth" label. There is a tendency for street youth to cycle between sleeping on the streets, shelters, squats, and low-quality housing several times before eventually maintaining housing for more extended periods of time.

It is also significant to acknowledge that, as is true with youth in general, street youth are at a time in their lives when they are incessantly seeking a sense of self and their environment, shifting in terms of identity and outlook, and acquiring understanding and knowledge. The process of exploring their relationship to information technology must be examined from within this context, for as youth cycle on and off the streets they are continually learning about themselves and the world around them. Learning comprises both the acquisition of particular knowledge sets and the process/experience of acquiring (Lindsey et al. 2000). In many ways, the development patterns of street youth reflect those of youth in mainstream society, albeit without the comfort of a safety net that is available to most young people.

Another contextual dimension that should be addressed is that street life is in itself a cultural arena and, as such, contains a particular set of values, norms, and mores that significantly affect youth when leaving the streets. The perception of street culture as isolating, deviant or criminal, and distinct from mainstream society presents significant challenges for young people as they attempt to bridge such separate worlds and regain a sense of citizenship in civil society.

It is important to remember that this population should be understood first as young people—adolescents—who in many ways exhibit characteristics similar to their mainstream cohorts: they are spirited, adventurous, resilient, and searching for and carving out a space for themselves within their environments. There is a significant difference about these young people, however. Street youth are a traumatized group; they are spiritually, physically, and emotionally unhealthy and have experienced unimaginable scenarios of exploitation, neglect, abuse, and suffering at the hands of both caregivers and civil society in general (Green 1998; Karabanow 2004; Panter-Brick and Smith 2000; Weber 1991). As such, the research concerning street youth and their relationships with the modern world becomes all the more important in order to support and advocate for this very marginalized population.

METHODOLOGY

In-depth qualitative interviews were conducted with twenty young people, aged 16 to 21 years, living on the street and/or in youth shelter/supportive housing in Halifax, Nova Scotia. Halifax is a mid-size coastal city on the eastern shores of Canada. Out of the twenty youth interviewed, fourteen were male (70%) and six were female.[1] Seventy percent of the sample had lived in Nova Scotia their entire lives. Street youth were invited to participate in the research study through advertisements situated in two local service agencies and through word of mouth. Each young person was offered fifteen dollars to complete an interview. Interview questions were semi-structured and explored young people's experiences with various technologies in terms of interactions, perceptions, comfortability, access, and knowledge. In order to complement the qualitative narratives, a quantitative survey was administered to participants that posed similar queries in the form of closed-ended questions and gathered information on demographic variables.

Qualitative data analysis involved open, axial, and selective coding techniques that encompassed fracturing of the data into conceptually specific themes and categories, rebuilding the data in new ways by linking primary categories and auxiliary themes into a path analysis, and constructing a theoretical narrative shaped by data integration and category construction (Strauss and Corbin 1990). The quantitative data was organized using basic descriptive frequencies.

One of the reasons we chose to interview those on the street and in more stable living arrangements (such as shelters and supportive housing structures) is to begin to explore the experiences and insights of both hard-core street youth and those situated within the street-exiting process (Karabanow, 2004). As such, although it seems reasonable to suspect that those in more stable settings would have some familiarity and access to ICT-related activities, it was also noted that street-entrenched young people have similar interests and encounters with computer technology. In fact, these two diverse street youth populations shared very similar experiences in general.

FEELING CONNECTED

Historically, of course, the Internet represents a major development as an electronic communication medium, analogous to earlier technologies such as the telegraph, radio, and telephone. The Internet as a technological tool, however, can be seen to depart from these other ICTs in new and novel ways by not only compressing but extending time and space, allowing asynchronous communication possibilities to take place at undetermined times and sequences (Castells 2001). While remaining a constituent dimension of earlier ICT trajectories and developments (Thrift 1996), the Internet offers different social ways to interact (Veenhof 2006). For instance, how street youth in our sample use ICTs capitalizes on the communication possibilities created through now seemingly ubiquitous tools such as email, leveraging new ways to stay in touch and communicate in the otherwise potentially risky or unstable relationships associated with street youth life.

The vast majority of the sample reported incorporating ICT-related activities in their daily lives. Although there has been very little research exploring street youth experiences with ICTs, this study highlights a surprising finding—the majority of the street-youth sample used computers either daily or at least several times per week. On average, participants spent 6.5 hours on the computer per week, primarily on the Internet. This is an astounding figure when we consider that a recent Statistics Canada study classified "heavy internet users" as those who spend on average an hour or more per day of personal time on the Internet (Veenhof 2006). What makes this figure even more impressive is that the street-youth population is one that fits within any definition of the "digital divide," whether we define the digital divide in terms of equal access (Canada 2001) or gaps in socio-economic status (OECD 2001). In this respect, it becomes important to explore and attend to *how* street youth experience the "feelings of connection" offered by ICTs, since it this capacity of connecting through ICTs that they primarily leverage when accessing a computer.

The street youth interviewed in this study reported generally that through the communication capacities offered by the Internet they felt more connected. Surprisingly, street youth and those in supportive housing spoke of feeling at ease with ICTs—lacking discomfort or overwhelming feelings using computer programs or learning new computer skills. Youth made statements such as, "I feel more connected for sure," "You can find out what's going on in the world," and "I feel more in touch with the world" to demonstrate their attitude toward the Internet. Speaking to the communication capacities of the Internet, one youth summed it up by saying, "It's like you've got instant power at your fingertips pretty much." For the most part, these young people used computers for email activity—connecting with friends and family. In our sample, the Internet was primarily used for email (37%) and instant messaging (26%), while 40% of participants primarily played games on the computer. As such, to our suprise, these youth have both computer skills (for such activities as email, Internet activity, job and apartment searches, and resumé creation) and frequent computer interaction. For many, the only inter-actions these young people had with family members involved email discus-sions. As many youth suggested, email use was a more cost-efficient and immediate forum by which to connect, especially considering the marginal status of this population. One youth pointed out, "I still think they [comput-ers] play a major role in the life of a homeless person. Just because they don't have a computer it doesn't mean they don't know how to use them or enjoy using them whenever they can. They probably don't play as big a role in their life as in the life of someone that owns a computer of course but still, they can keep in touch with their friends and stuff like that. They're still a regular per-son, they just don't have a computer."

Although a homeless person may still be a "regular person," being home-less is definitively marked by a differentiated set of psycho-social factors. It is often associated with a sense of failure, feelings of helplessness caused by the inability to secure basic needs, and by familial and social isolation and ostracism (Cohen, Putnam and Sullivan 1984). As Rokach (2005, 476) notes, the lit-erature is clear that "relocating to the street is probably a sure way of losing important relationships, and transience of living necessarily brings with it transient social connections." For homeless youth, caring, trustworthy, and supportive close relationships are very important, but maintaining close rela-tionships with family and friends can prove exceedingly difficult, particularly since adolescent runaways and homelessness may include a chaotic home life marked by disruption, abuse, and conflict (Rokach 2005). In our view, our sample's heightened use of the computer to access the Internet for communi-cation purposes tentatively suggests that it is being used as a coping tool for youth in their street careers. When considering the obstacles to access for this population, who identify themselves as a marginal and alienated subculture (Karabanow 2004; Green 1998; Michaud 1989; Miller et al. 1980), their per-severance in gaining access to and exploiting the communication features of ICTs appears remarkable. Asked about his computer use now that he was out of the home, one respondent noted that "I use them a lot more because I've got-ten reconnected with my family when I got kicked out and stuff. Now I can go and do whatever I want, you know without my parents always being on my back and stuff. I'm more free to just like go to the library and check my email."

Typical of comments from our sample, who reported feeling more connected through the Internet, as well as a heavy investment of time, this comment suggests that despite inequalities around access for marginalized populations, street youth are engaging ICTs as an exploitative coping strategy for life on the street and out of the home. Moreover, many participants suggested that computer use was a way to pass time and stay out of trouble. Instead of engaging in illegal or delinquent street activities, computer involvement allowed many young people an enticing and legitimate option. As one youth stated, "Well, you can stay out of trouble ... if you had a computer and you're playing for hours and hours, you wouldn't be doing stupid stuff." Previous research has identified the notion of boredom that plagues street youth populations and at times can induce criminal and/or deviant behavior (Karabanow 2004; Karabanow et al. 2005; McCarthy 1990); the use of ICTs may in fact reduce such involvement, which suggests the need for increased opportunities and access to computer use. There is some evidence that computing activities also act as safe refuges for those living in stressful environments (Tsikalas, Gross, and Stock 2003). Numerous participants suggest that time spent with computers enabled them to escape or disengage from their street identities: "It's kind of nice because you can just kind of be yourself and not really worry about how people look at you ... you can just sort of be yourself."

In conceptualizing ICT use, evidenced through the communication capacities of the Internet explored here, it is possible to suggest that street youth see ICTs as a means to feel connected in their lives in ways that other technologies do not permit, and in ways that are novel to our understanding of street youth careers. That said, we would caution against understanding ICT as a solution to the complex problems of homelessness, and here we take care to distance ourselves from understanding ICTs as a communications panacea, expressed commonly through positive orientations expressed in metaphors of highway, surfing, or play. The experiences and understandings of homeless youth with ICTs lack any meaning without reference to their everyday lives. As Sassen (2002, 368) reminds us, "Digital space is embedded in the larger societal, cultural, subjective, economic, imaginary structurations of lived experience and the systems within which we exist and operate." While more research is needed to investigate the possibilities of connectedness for street youth through ICTs, we can surmise that ICTs amount to a potentially powerful tool in the lives of street youth, yet one that remains contested by virtue of its embeddedness in the material conditions of social marginality and rejection associated with homeless youth.

STREET YOUTH AND ICT LITERACY

Now an ever-present term of popular media, business, and government, the notion of a knowledge economy is an attempt to conceptually depict new processes where *knowledge about technology* and levels of information flow become fundamental to individual and socio-economic development (OECD 1996). To this end, there is now a significant contention that *literacy with ICTs* represents a major obstacle to overcome for both capital and labour in advanced economies if they are to compete globally as a "knowledge economy." Within Canada a range of resources and efforts aimed at increasing ICT literacy in mainstream domains such as education and training have been allocated within the past decade. If we begin with the assumption that access to ICTs is crucial to today's knowledge economy, exploring street youth's attitudes and understandings of ICTs becomes essential, in this context, at the peril of confining an already marginalized population to become further "left behind." particularly given the current emphasis on the links between ICT literacy, employment and economic success. To continue to ignore street youth experiences with ICTs risks not only deepening an already deep digital divide, then, but also denying that one exists altogether. When we consider the connection, however, between ICT literacy, pathways to success, and street youth, the link becomes extremely tenuous. For instance, many homeless and at-risk youth lack basic employment skills (Karabanow et al. 2005), and a lack of interest in personal well-being is often associated with being homeless (Layton 2000).

Although less integral than finding food or a place to stay, the majority of our sample surprisingly perceived ICTs as a fairly major activity within their street careers. As our discussion above suggests, these young people had intimate knowledge of technology through previous experiences with family and/or school and found time daily or weekly to maintain some involvement with ICT activity. The majority of young people interviewed also spoke of having some comfort and ease with ICTs (approximately 70% of participants self-assess their computer abilities as better than average; 85% of the sample suggest a comfortability with computers), much of it stemming from previous elementary and high school experiences (the majority of the sample is currently out of school) and/or learning from a family member. The mean sam-

ple age of first using a computer was eleven years old (twelve years old for first
Internet use). Although the majority employed ICTs for email use, many also
spoke of job/apartment searching, resumé development, game playing, downloading music, and searching for particular information, suggesting some
depth to their ICT literacy. Interestingly, participants did not use computers
to search out services/programs for homeless youth or general information
concerning homelessness, instead relying on word of mouth to access such
specific service-delivery structures.

Evidence from this study identifies the importance of ICT use and
access from the perspectives of young homeless people. A majority of participants are keenly aware of the need to become computer literate in order to
take advantage of what can be offered via such technologies (such as word
processing, email, Internet searches, and resumé writing) and, equally important, become competitive employees within the current knowledge-economy
nexus. One participant commented, "technology is becoming the way every-
body does everything nowadays; it's becoming part of the world. If you don't
know it, you might get lost." Another young person suggested, "I think you
can't be computer illiterate nowadays because computers are everything."

It is not surprising that young people living on the street identify themselves as constituents of marginal and alienated subcultures (Karabanow 2004;
Green 1998; Michaud 1989; Miller et al. 1980); however, it is significant that
a majority perceive the importance of technology know-how (i.e., ICT literacy) if they are to eke out fruitful and meaningful employment in the future.
As such, ICT use and access are important issues facing homeless youth in
terms of reducing *feelings* of "being left behind" and being left behind in real
terms with respect to mainstream ICT adoption. Statistics Canada (2004)
reports that Internet use is highest at home (about 6.7 million households
had at least one member who regularly used the Internet from home), a fact
not particularly encouraging for the homeless. In addition, Statistics Canada
(2004) reports that households with high income, members active in the
labour force, and people with high levels of education remain at the vanguard
of Internet adoption in Canada. Given these patterns, it is clear that street
youth remain dangerously marginalized as users of ICTs. Although more study
is needed to explore the links between homeless youth and ICT literacy, however, it is possible to conclude that homeless youth do take ICT literacy seriously, and our sample clearly recognized its importance to any potential career
or future advancement.

ACCESS

The use of ICTs by street youth to cope and communicate as a way of feeling "hooked up," coupled with their recognition of the importance of ICT literacy, suggests ICTs are a surprisingly robust feature in the street careers of the youth in our sample. When we begin to examine issues of access to ICTs for street youth in terms of simple contact with ICTs we find access problematic. The majority of our sample lived on the street and/or in a local shelter/supportive-housing complex, where access to computer technologies proved limited and constrained: "Sometimes I don't have any access at all and it's hard, when I really, really need to use a computer." Many of the young people interviewed, however, spoke of a local downtown drop-in service which allowed computer use during operating hours. The drop-in centre was primarily a popular service for food, counselling, showers, and washing clothes, but nonetheless employed three modern computers that could be accessed by clients on a first-come, first-served basis. Street youth highlighted the importance of such a service that allowed them mostly unregulated computer use, with workers available to provide any technical support: "Here they help you out. We can come in and say we need help or anything and they'll come over and help us and tell us you know, this is the best way to do it and stuff and it's really good."

For young people living in a residential shelter, computers could be used through the organization's learning and employment centre; although somewhat more regulated (as to what sites/activities could be accessed), this provided ample opportunity to familiarize oneself with ICTs. Moreover, this learning and employment centre provided regular computer workshops on such topics as resumé writing, job searching, and accessing the Internet. The majority of the sample felt much gratitude for these two homeless-youth service providers for allowing young people the ability to become (or continue to be) computer literate. Although some youth accessed computers through friends or family on an irregular basis, the vast majority experienced frequent computer use through the shelter and/or drop-in settings.

A second avenue for computer access came from a local downtown public library (C@P Site) where young people could access one of five computers set up for public use. Although limited in terms of having to present personal identification (or library card), hours of operation, long waits, not being allowed to download or print, and having certain restrictions on site searches, many street youth frequently used the library as a way to check/send emails and search for jobs/accommodations. Speaking about access and restriction issues, one youth suggested, "There should be, I don't really know but maybe there should be places where there's a larger number of computers and maybe a little more freedom that people have when they're at home rather than being told what they're allowed to do. You know there's always limits on what you're allowed to look at and do on computers."

A number of young people shared their frustrations with not having personal freedom on a library computer (as one would have with one's own computer) and the often-long waits for computer access. Nevertheless the library still provided street youth with a free opportunity to access computer technologies. One youth noted, "With all these C@P sites that they have around, they should have several more of those [computers]. Plus the public libraries, you should not have to use your library card to log on because it makes it a lot harder for youth who have nothing to do throughout the day but want to go in and learn things."

The majority of participants highlight the fact that when homeless youth services and local libraries are closed, there is little avenue by which these young people can engage in computer activity. Such a finding not only gives credence to services that involve young people with computer activity but also argues for increased access so that young people on the street do not become left behind vis-à-vis the emerging knowledge economy.

Although physical access to ICTs remains a key divide to digital access, many analysts of the digital divide now emphasize the importance of not simply seeing the digital divide as a one dimensional problem reduced and solved by simply providing ICT and connectivity access to those without. Indeed, as Parayil (2005, 41) observes, "The digital divide is often portrayed in crassly reductive terms as a mere technological access that can be ostensibly addressed by providing cheap computing and communication technologies to the poor." Rather, it is essential to see ICTs as part of social process that is dynamic and complex and that social inclusion around ICT "does not exist as an external variable to be injected from the outside to bring about certain results" (Warschauer 2002, 6). With respect to street youth, recognizing that their experiences with ICTs remain marginal and situated locally within an existing web of social services, organizations, and processes, we deepen our understanding of their relation to ICT by reminding ourselves that street youth participants exist within domains of social exclusion and inclusion vis-à-vis their interactions with ICTs. On one hand, this research suggests that these street youth are in fact "citizens" of technology through their comfort and ease with computers; however, this sense of citizenship is ephemeral when faced with issues of accessibility as well as the larger context of street survival. For instance, several street youth suggested that ICTs had only a minor impact on their lives, which for the most part involved meeting basic needs (i.e., shelter, food, clothing, and money): "the main thing for me is getting through the day." Another youth noted, "Most homeless people have more important things to think about like getting off the streets, not playing on computers." These kinds of comments remind us that simple access to ICTs for street youth, while helpful, will not bridge the digital divide in ways that necessarily improve equity or social inclusiveness. As noted by a service provider at one of the organizations that support street youth access to computers, "They [street youth] are isolated, so technology doesn't suddenly mean that they are not isolated, but it doesn't mean that they are less. I just mean in terms of education and school and society. It's not the technology that's isolating them. They're isolated period or we have isolated them as a community. And their proficiency in technology does not mean that they are no longer isolated."

Recognizing that street youths' experiences with ICTs are embedded within the complexity of their everyday lived experiences requires us to consider the wider social context of their relationship to ICT: "The big problem with 'the digital divide' framing is that it tends to connote 'digital solutions,' i.e., computers and telecommunications, without engaging the important set of complementary resources and complex interventions to support social inclusion, of which informational technology applications may be enabling elements, but are certainly insufficient when simply added to the status quo mix of resources and relationships" (Kling, quoted in Warschauer 2002, 6).

In this context, future research needs to explore whether ICTs can act as an agent of change for young people to support their transitions out of homelessness and into adequate employment and safe housing, or whether they act simply as short-term distractions from the misery of being homeless. What appears clear from the data is that this street-youth sample uses ICT predominantly for bonding social capital purposes—connecting with people who are familiar to them (i.e., family and friends). The finding that these young people actually engage in ICT use within their day to day activities could, however, be understood as glimpses of bridging social capital (linking with diverse others) through the connection between social exclusion (i.e., street youth) and information technology (i.e., mainstream apparatus). In this light, the interplay between street youth and information technology demonstrates both bridging and bonding social capital elements—young people forming ties within subgroups and across groups. Future research will need to explore whether ICT use supports (or even precipitates) a young person's transformation from an identity of exclusion (i.e., being a street youth) to an identity of inclusion (i.e., moving into mainstream society). If so, how does this process of bridging the divide between street life and mainstream culture actually take place? Moreover, we contend that if ICT is to act as more than just another coping or job-search strategy, effective as it may be, efforts must be made to incorporate the full experience of homeless street youth into any effort to employ ICT as a means to social inclusion. In other words, future analyses can help define whether such technologies in fact bridge the digital divide in the broadest sense or simply deepen it.

CONCLUSION

There has been little discussion of street youths' interpretations and experiences vis-à-vis ICTs; rather, the vast majority of literature has investigated how young people enter and survive street life. This study of twenty street youth in Halifax Nova Scotia, explores how young people interact, experience, and access ICTs in their day-to-day street existence. Surprisingly, findings demonstrate that this population was in daily or weekly contact with ICT-related activities including email, Internet search, job/housing search, and resumé creation. Apart from the daily stresses of finding shelter, food, clothing, and other basic needs, these street youth were interested and knowledgeable about computer activities.

The majority of participants felt comfortable and at ease with computer work and were keenly aware of the importance of information technologies within the current global economic structure. ICTs were primarily used to make life easier for them on the street and involved connecting (or reconnecting) with family and friends, searching out employment and housing, developing a resumé, and searching out particular information via the Internet. In addition, like many of their counterparts in mainstream society, computers were a source of enjoyment and passing time. Numerous participants suggested that computer use was directly associated with less involvement in criminal and/or delinquent street activities—providing rather a space for recreation and personal development. Access to computers was primarily achieved through local youth services and a downtown public library. Although these avenues did provide youth with significant computer interaction, a majority of the sample noted a desire for increased access to information technologies that meet the needs of those who are homeless and living on the street. Such a recommendation may prove highly significant if future research demonstrates a correlation between ICT use/access and reduction of deviant and dangerous street activities.

Finally, it was surprising to explore the keen insights of these young people in terms of how important computer literacy was in the face of an increasing technology-driven knowledge economy—again raising the issue of computer access for marginalized groups. The majority of our sample suggested that knowledge of ICTs could lead to more fruitful and exciting employment in the future, which perhaps explains why such an alienated population continues to maintain frequent computer involvement even in the face of such degradation as living on the street.

NOTE

1   A limitation of the study is that the sample was made up of those who volunteered to be part of this investigation and is not representative of the broader population of street youth. Given the focus of the research on ICTs, the youth who participated may well be those most interested in and involved with ICT.

WORKS CITED

Castells, M. 2000. *The Rise of the Network Society.* 2nd edition. Malden, MA: Blackwell.

Child Welfare League of America. 1991. "Homelessness: The Impact on Child Welfare in the '90s." Washington, DC: Child Welfare League of America.

Cohen, N., J. Putnam, and A. Sullivan. 1984. "The Mentally Ill Homeless: Isolation and Adaptation." *Hospital and Community Psychiatry* 35:922–24.

Eamon, M.K. 2004. "Digital Divide in Computer Access and Use Between Poor and Non-Poor Youth." *Journal of Sociology and Social Welfare* 31:91–112.

Edelbrock, C. 1980. "Running Away from Home: Incidence and Correlates among Children and Youth Referred for Mental Health Services." *Journal of Family Issues* 1:210–28.

Eng, J. 1994. "Even the Homeless Find Welcome Mat on the Internet." *Vancouver Sun.* Vancouver.

Fitzgerald, M. 1998. "To Live and Learn: Homeless Youth, Literacy, Education and Career." Halifax, NS: Phoenix Youth Programs.

Green, D. 1998. *Hidden Lives: Voices of Children in Latin America and the Caribbean.* Toronto: Between the Lines.

Halifax Regional Municipality. 2004. *Homelessness in HRM: Portraits of Streets and Shelter.* Halifax, NS: Planning and Development Services.

Halifax Regional Municipality. 2005. *Homelessness in HRM: Portraits of Streets and Shelter, Vol. II.* Halifax, NS: Planning and Development Services.

Janus, M., A. McCormack, A. Burgess, and C. Hartman. 1987. "Adolescent Runaways—Causes and Consequences." Lexington, MA: Lexington Books.

Karabanow, J. 2003. "Creating a Culture of Hope: Lessons from Street Children Agencies in Canada and Guatemala." *International Social Work* 46:369–86.

———. 2004. *Being Young and Homeless: Understanding How Youth Enter and Exit Street Life.* New York: Peter Lang.

———. 2008. "Getting off the Street: Exploring Young People's Street Exits." *American Behavioral Scientist* 51:772–88.

Karabanow, J, Clement, P., A. Carson, and K. Crane. 2005. "Getting Off the Street: Exploring Strategies Used by Canadian Youth to Exit Street Life." Ottawa: National Research Program.

Kufeldt, K. and M. Nimmo. 1987. "Youth on the Street." *Child Abuse and Neglect* 11:531–43.

Layton, J. 2000. *Homelessness: The Making and Unmaking of a Crisis.* Toronto: Penguin.

Lindsey, E.W., P.D. Kurtz, S. Jarvis, N.R. Williams, and L. Nackerud. 2000. "How Runaway and Homeless Youth Navigate Troubled Waters: Personal Strengths and Resources." *Child and Adolescent Social Work Journal* 17:115–40.

Looker, D. and V. Thiessen. 2003. "Beyond the Digital Divide in Canadian Schools: From Access to Competency in the Use of Information Technology." *Social Science Computer Review* 21:475–90.

McCarthy, W. 1990 "Life on the Streets," PhD thesis, Sociology, University of Toronto.

Michaud, M. 1988. *Dead End.* Calgary: Detselig Enterprises.

Miller, D., D. Miller, F. Hoffman, and R. Duggan. 1980. *Runaways: Illegal Aliens in Their Own Land.* Santa Barbara, CA: Praeger.

Milton, P. 2003, "Trends in the Integration of ICT and Learning in K–12 Systems." Toronto, ON: Canadian Education Association. http://www.cea-ace.ca/media/en/Trends_ICT_Integration.pdf.

Morrissette, P. and S. McIntyre. 1989. "Homeless Youth in Residential Care." *Social Casework* 20:165–88.

Murray, M. 1995. "Up Front: Putting a Byte on the Street-wise." *Toronto Star.* Toronto.

Organization for Economic Co-operation and Development. 1996, "The Knowledge-based Economy." http://www.oecd.org/dataoecd/51/8/1913021.pdf.

———. 2001. "Understanding the Digital Divide." http://www.oecd.org/dataoecd/38/57/1888451.pdf.

Panter-Brick, C. and M. Smith. 2000. *Abandoned Children.* Cambridge: Cambridge University Press.

Parayil, G. 2005. "The Digital Divide and Increasing Returns: Contradictions of Informational Capitalism." *The Information Society* 21:41–51.

Pearson, T. 2002. "Falling Behind: A Technology Crisis Facing Minority Students." *TechTrends* 46:15–20.

Raffaelli, M. and R. Larson. 1999. *Homeless and Working Youth Around the World: Exploring Developmental Issues*. San Francisco: Jossey-Bass.

Robertson, M. and M. Greenblatt. 1992. *Homelessness: A National Perspective*. New York: Plenum Press.

Rokach, A. 2005. "The Causes of Loneliness in Homeless Youth." *The Journal of Psychology* 139:469–80.

Sassen, S. 2002. "Towards a Sociology of Information Technology." *Current Sociology* 50:365–88.

Shane, P. 1989. "Changing Patterns among Homeless and Runaway Youth." *American Journal of Orthopsychiatry* 59:208–14.

Statistics Canada. 2004. "Household Internet Use Survey," 8 July. http://www.statcan .ca/Daily/English/040708/d040708a.htm.

Stierlin, H. 1973. "Family Perspectives on Adolescent Runaways." *Archives of General Psychiatry* 29:56–62.

Strauss, A. and J. Corbin. 1990. *Basics of Qualitative Research*. Newbury Park, CA: Sage.

Thrift, N. 1996. "New Urban Eras and Old Technological Fears: Reconfiguring the Goodwill of Electronic Things." *Urban Studies* 33:1463–93.

Tsikalas, K., E. Gross, and E. Stock. 2002. "Applying a Youth Psychology Lens to the Digital Divide: How Low-income, Minority Adolescents Appropriate Home Computers to Meet Their Needs for Autonomy, Belonging and Competence, and How This Affects Their Academic and Future Prospects." Paper presented at the Annual Meeting of the American Educational Research Association, New Orleans, LA. 1–5 April.

van der Ploeg, J.D. 1989. "Homelessness: A Multidimensional Problem." *Children and Youth Services Review* 11:45–56.

Veenhof, B. 2006. "The Internet: Is It Changing the Way Canadians Spend Their Time?" Ottawa: Statistics Canada, Science, Innovation and Electronic Information Division (SIEID).

Warschauer, M. 2002. "Reconceptualizing the Digital Divide." *First Monday* 7:1–17.

Weber, M. 1991. *Street Kids*. Toronto: University of Toronto Press.

Yablonsky, L. 1968. *The Hippie Trip*. New York, NY: Pegasus.

Contributors

Brian Lewis Campbell is a sociologist who is interested in the sociology of science and technology and the sociology of education. These general interests have come together in the study of technology diffusion and translation in education with special attention to the relationship between information technology use and social inequality. Campbell is a professor in the Faculty of Social Sciences and Humanities at University of Ontario Institute of Technology (UOIT) but spends most of his time as associate provost and dean of graduate studies.

Blye W. Frank is a professor and head of the Division of Medical Education and the head of the Department of Bioethics in the Faculty of Medicine at Dalhousie University. He has worked with faculties of medicine and health professions across Canada toward the promotion of diversity and cultural competency in the medical/health education environment. He is also a recognized expert in the field of gender studies. Dr. Frank is chair of the CIHR Institute of Gender and Health Institute Advisory Board.

Alyssa Henning was a research assistant in the Equity and Technology Research Alliance project on digital divide issues. She has a B.A. in criminology and justice studies from the University of Ontario Institute of Technology and an M.A. in public policy and administration from Ryerson University. She now works in the public sector in project coordination for non-profit agencies.

Jeff Karabanow is a full professor at Dalhousie University. He has worked with homeless young people in Toronto, Montreal, Halifax, and Guatemala. He has published numerous academic articles about housing stability, service delivery systems, street health, and homeless youth culture. He has also completed a film documentary that looks at the plight of street youth in Guatemala City and two animated shorts on street life in Canada. His most recent work is a book titled *Voices from the Streets: How Canadian Homeless Young People are Getting Off the Street* (forthcoming).

E. Dianne Looker, professor of Sociology and Canada Research Chair in Equity and Technology at Mount Saint Vincent University, has undertaken several longitudinal surveys dealing with youth in a changing society, with particular focus on rural–urban differences. She has provided expert advice to numerous policy groups and government departments. Her recent work looks at ways in which the shift to a more information society has affected equity for subgroups of youth in Canada and abroad.

Ted D. Naylor is a research manager and associate with the Atlantic Centre for the Study of the Information Society, Mount Saint Vincent University. A mixed-methods researcher with a diverse publication record, Naylor works on a variety of research projects in both the public and private sector. He is currently completing an interdisciplinary Ph.D. at Dalhousie University.

Victor Thiessen is professor emeritus in the Department of Sociology and Social Anthropology, Dalhousie University, and academic director of the Atlantic Research Data Centre. His work in the past twenty years has focused on youth transitions, an area in which he has published extensively. His current investigations focus on the various pathways along which young Canadians navigate their way from schooling to employment.

Index